GERMAN NAVAL VESSELS OF WORLD WAR TWO

German Naval Vessels of World War Two

Compiled by US Naval Intelligence

Introduction by A. D. Baker III

Naval Institute Press
Annapolis, Maryland

Published and distributed in the United States of America
by the Naval Institute Press, Annapolis, Maryland 21402.

This edition is authorized for sale only in the
United States and its territories and possessions.

Library of Congress Catalog Card No. 93-83888

ISBN 1-55750-304-4

Printed and bound in Hong Kong by Colorcraft Limited

TABLE OF CONTENTS

Introduction by A.D. Baker III   *Page 7*

World War II-Era ONI Recognition
    and Characteristics Publications   *11*

Notes on Sources   *12*

ONI 204 – German Naval Vessels

Charts

   1. Characteristics of German Naval Vessels

   2. German One-Stackers

   3. Jerry Jingles

   4. Recognition Similarities

   5. Naval Camouflage

List of German Naval Vessels

Range Table

Ships

BB-1	Gneisenau
BB-2	Scharnhorst
BB-4	Tirpitz
OBB-1, 2	Schleswig Holstein, Schlesien
CV-1	Graf Zeppelin
CA-1	Admiral Hipper
CA-3	Prinz Eugen
CA-6	Lützow
CA-7	Admiral Scheer
CL-1	Emden
CL-4	Köln
CL-5	Leipzig
CL-6	Nürnberg
DD-1-16	Maasz Class
DD-20	Karl Galster
DD-23-43	Narvik and New Classes
DD-44-55	Seizures

TB-1-6	Möwe Class	PG-1-10	F-1 Class
TB-7-12	Wolf Class	PG-19	Brummer
TB-13-42	T-1 Class	CD	Seizures
TB-43-46	Ex-Norwegian	PY-2	Grille
OTB-1-4	T-107 Class	PT-7-111	"S" Series
SS-740	Ton	TLC	Tank Landing Craft
SS-517	Ton	AVP	Seaplane Tenders
SS-250	Ton	AH	Hospital Ships
SS-300-500-1060	Ton		Ex-M Class
AM-27-66	M-1 Class		Trawlers
AMc-	R Class	SS & PC	Tenders
AM-CM	Seizures	AO - AE - AP - ACL	
AVC-1-4			

INTRODUCTION

When my ship entered the South China Sea on the way to Vietnamese waters in 1966, we had our first practical lesson in the importance of good ship recognition skills: two U.S. Navy ocean minesweepers passed us en route home for repairs, proudly inviting our attention to the scars in their wooden hulls received during a strafing attack by U.S. Air Force Phantom fighters. A few months later, during Market Time coastal patrols, we worked for a day or two with a U.S. Coast Guard-manned 82-foot cutter that was sunk shortly thereafter by U.S. aircraft claiming to have attacked an awash Russian or Chinese Whiskey-class submarine – in waters about thirty feet deep. Still later, while stationed in Washington D.C., I had occasion to inspect aerial photos of a U.S. Navy 'Nasty'-class fast patrol boat burned out after attack by our own forces.

Naval history is, of course, replete with other examples of misidentification leading to the loss of lives and ships. In recent times, for example, in 1974 the Turkish Air Force sank the Turkish destroyer *Koçatepe* (ex-U.S.S. *Harwood*, DD 859), having mistaken her for a similar Greek unit. It is ironic, however, that the Vietnam struggle brought out failures in United States forces' recognition training, for during World War II, the U.S. Navy brought recognition training to a state not equalled before or since by any other nation. Vietnam mistakes brought home the lesson that the age of the supersonic aircraft and the 'smart' bomb had not made it any less necessary to be able to distinguish friend from foe, or one foe from another.

For most of World War II, the U.S. Navy's Office of Naval Intelligence was not directly involved in operational intelligence, which, after several vicious and protracted bureaucratic turf wars, was held to be a prerogative of the operational forces. Thus, ONI was left free to devote itself to counterintelligence (which occupied the vast majority of its personnel) and technical intelligence, at which it had excelled since its founding in 1882 as the nation's first chartered government intelligence service.

Part of the work of ONI was the production of recognition and technical publications about our own and foreign ships and aircraft. The work that eventually resulted in books like

ONI 204, *German Naval Vessels*, had been begun by Lieutenant Arthur H. McCollum during a tour of duty as head of the ONI Japan desk in 1933-34 in Washington, D.C. McCollum pioneered the use of scale models photographed from various angles to produce recognition materials for use in a classified publication about the Imperial Japanese Navy – which was the principal perceived opponent for the U.S. Navy in the 1930s and which was experiencing a rapid and formidable growth.

When McCollum returned to ONI in 1939 as a lieutenant commander, he found that his earlier work had been forgotten and proceeded to start anew. The previously-built scale models were relocated after a six-month search, although the original builder had died. By 1941, McCollum was able to issue a new book describing and illustrating the Japanese fleet.

The Identification and Characteristics Section of ONI, OP-16-F-20, was established on 31 December 1941 under Commander Charles G. Moore to continue the efforts begun by McCollum and to broaden the scope to include additional navies. OP-16-F-20 was expected to use all available technical information, photography, line drawings, silhouettes, and model photography in its production of recognition materials. The section was staffed in large measure by highly-qualified Naval Reservists who in peacetime had worked as draftsmen and architects.

The ONI draftsmen developed the concept of employing a 'master drawing' of each significant ship class, modifying the drawing each time new information was received. Changes in the configuration of ships of the U.S. Navy were easily accommodated, for shipyards were required to supply ONI with small-scale plan and elevation drawings made after each yard period. The British Royal Navy went even further, providing reduced negatives of actual Admiralty 'As-Fitted' general arrangement plans for ONI use in making recognition drawings. Drawings and photographs of ships of the belligerent navies, however, were harder to come by, and not a few photos that had been clipped from the pages of a pre-war *Jane's Fighting Ships* found their way into ONI manuals; most of the line drawings had to be painstakingly prepared through use of the available photography.

The models used in illustrating ONI's recognition manuals were initially built at the David Taylor Model Basin in Carderock, Maryland, and later by Van Ryper, a professional model-builder who resided on Martha's Vineyard, a small island off the southern coast of Cape Cod in Massachusetts. Photos of the finished models were taken from various surface and aerial target angles and were provided, along with line drawings, shaded airbrush drawings, photography, and texts to Time, Incorporated, which did the actual printing and layout under contract; the use of the commercial publishing house guaranteed the high standard of printing and layout and the production facilities needed to make the books useful as training aids. Also produced by the Identification and Characteristics Section were other visual aids such as wall charts and decks of flash cards depicting ships and aircraft.

The initial editions of the various ONI manuals, like ONI

204, were devoted primarily to graphic presentations. By 1943, however, more and more technical data had become available, not only about the ships but also about the equipment and weapons they carried. At the same time, the use of airbrush drawings and model photos was discontinued, and standard plan and elevation line drawings and additional photography were substituted. By war's end, most of the major volumes in the ONI series of recognition books had run through at least two editions, with the earlier editions expected to be destroyed and replaced by the newer products, which tended to be on $8\frac{1}{2}$ by 11-inch paper rather than in the earlier landscape format.

The ONI Identification and Characteristics Section's span of responsibilities gradually broadened as the war went on until it ran the gamut of what today is called 'Scientific and Technical' intelligence, and more and more professionally trained scientists and engineers were required to carry out its tasks. Accordingly, ONI formed the Technical Intelligence Center in October 1944 to take over the detailed work of technical intelligence, by which time the Identification and Characteristics Section itself had already transferred its art and layout staff to the ONI Publications Branch, leaving I&C Section to concentrate on processing and evaluating the deluge of data becoming available as the Allies began to overrun Axis territories. The I&C Section had also been involved in the monthly joint services *Recognition Journal* (again, with publications services contracted to Time, Incorporated) and had also made a major contribution to the production of the joint Army and Navy J.A.N. No. 1, *Uniforms and Insignia*.

Post World War II, as the Naval Intelligence function first shrank drastically and then began to grow again as attention became focused on the threat arising from the Soviet Union, recognition came to be thought of as a *training* function divorced from the production of technical intelligence about foreign naval capabilities. ONI continued post-war to produce technical intelligence about foreign naval capabilities. ONI continued post-war to produce technical manuals (the ONI 32 series) about foreign fleets, illustrating them with photography and shaded line drawings, but the volumes were classified 'secret' and were thus of almost no use to the fleet for training the majority of personnel in the skills of ship recognition. By the 1950s, the Bureau of Personnel (BUPERS) was in charge of issuing recognition slide sets and manuals, the quality of which was a distinct cut below the work of ONI in the 1940s.

Since the late 1960s, the Naval Scientific and Technical Intelligence Center (the lineal descendant of the wartime Technical Intelligence Center and itself later renamed the Naval Intelligence Support Center and still later the Naval Maritime Intelligence Center when the technical and operational intelligence activities of ONI were at last brought together under one command) has continued to produce similar but more detailed classified manuals for the Defense Intelligence Agency, the *Naval Ships Characteristics Handbooks* series. After the Vietnam War had proved the need for better recognition training materials, Naval Intelligence once again took up the task of providing recognition guides, but they were not anywhere near the same quality as those produced half a century earlier.

ONI 204, *German Naval Vessels* was a product of the initial, McCollum-inspired era of ONI recognition materials, heavily dependent on visual aids such as silhouettes, beautifully shaded airbrush renderings, model photos (including some with salient details highlighted), and – to a lesser extent – photography of the actual ships. The ship photos were mostly of pre-war vintage, but a number of British-supplied wartime views were incorporated, and even a few German propaganda photographs that showed *Reichsmarine* ships in action. The volume's concern was with teaching the user to recognize instantly and from any angle the type and class of naval vessel encountered; the niceties of distinguishing between individual units within all but the most significant capital ship classes were beyond its scope. It was far more important that aviation and shipboard personnel be able to tell that a threat was in view.

ONI 204 carries a humorous bonus in the form of a cartoon by the famous U.S. Marine Corps author and artist, Colonel John W. Thomason, showing the importance of recognition readiness.

In addition to its visual impact as an outstanding example of the use of a wide variety of graphic arts to impart skills in recognition training, ONI 204 also fulfills its aim of depicting the numerous German-built and captured warships under *Reichsmarine* control. Regardless of the evil to which they were put, the Nazi-era warships were uniformly handsome vessels, and the book does them justice through its numerous illustrations. Ironically, even by the time that ONI 204 was issued, the majority of the German major surface combatants had been destroyed or neutralized in port, but that does not diminish the book's utility as a historical reference nor the enjoyment of its skillful and profligate use of all possible means of illustration.

A.D. Baker, III
1993

World War II-Era ONI Recognition and Characteristics Publications

JAN # 1:   *Uniforms and Insignia*[1]

ONI 54 series: *U.S. Naval Vessels*[2]

ONI 41-42:   *Japanese Naval Vessels*[3]

ONI 41-42:   *Recognition Supplement: Aerial Views of Japanese Naval Vessels*

ONI 201:   *Naval Vessels of the British Commonwealth*

ONI 202:   *Italian Naval Vessels*

ONI 203:   *French Naval Vessels*

ONI 204:   *German Naval Vessels*[4]

ONI 205-235:   *Russian Naval Vessels and Military Aircraft*

ONI 206:   *Minor European Navies*

ONI 208J: *Japanese Merchant Vessels*

ONI 208R: *Russian Merchant Vessels*

ONI 220M: *Axis Submarines*

ONI 222:   *Statistical Data on Foreign Navies*

ONI 223:   *Ship Shapes – Types and Anatomy of Naval Vessels*

ONI 223K: *Warships in Code*

ONI 223M: *Merchant Ship Shapes*

ONI 225J: *Japanese Landing Operations and Equipment*

ONI 226:   *Allied Landing Craft*[5]

ONI 232:   *Japanese Military Aircraft*

ONI 233:   *Italian Military Aircraft*

ONI 234:   *German Military Aircraft*

[1] Naval uniform sections extracted and published as *Uniforms & Insignia of the Navies of World War II – As Seen by U.S. Naval Intelligence*, London & Annapolis, Md., 1991.

[2] November 1943 edition published as *U.S. Naval Vessels 1943*, London & Annapolis, Md., 1986.

[3] Published as *Japanese Naval Vessels of World War II – As Seen by U.S. Naval Intelligence*, London & Annapolis, Md., 1987, including also ONI 41-42, *Index to All Japanese Naval Vessels* (Dec. 1944), ONI-41-42, *Japanese Naval Vessels* (9 November 1942), ONI 220J, *Japanese Submarines* (undated, but probably 1942), and ONI 225J, *Japanese Landing Operations and Equipment* (21 May 1943).

[4] ONI 204, *German Naval Vessels* published as *German Naval Vessels of World War Two*, London & Annapolis, Md., 1993.

[5] June 1941 edition, with 1945 supplement, published as *Allied Landing Craft of World War II*, London & Annapolis, Md., 1985.

Notes on Sources

Information about the founding of the U.S. Navy recognition training effort is available in Volume 1 of the U.S. Naval Institute Oral History Collection's 1970-71 interviews with Rear Admiral Arthur H. McCollum, USN (1898-1976), access to which can be obtained through the U.S. Naval Institute, 118 Maryland Ave., Annapolis, MD 21402-5035 or at the Naval Historical Center, Operational Archives Branch, Building 57, Washington Navy Yard, Washington, DC 20374-0571; copies of the transcript are also maintained at the Nimitz Library, Special Collections, U.S. Naval Academy, Annapolis, MD 21402-1390, and at the Naval Historical Collection, Mahan Hall, Naval War College, Newport, RI 02841-5010. Detailed information about the ONI Identification and Characteristics Section will be found in the forthcoming history of U.S. Naval Intelligence by Captain Wyman H. Packard, USN (Ret.) to be published by the U.S. Government Printing Office under the auspices of the Office of Naval Intelligence and the Naval Historical Center.

A.D.B.

ONI 204—GERMAN NAVAL VESSELS

1. ONI 204—German Naval Vessels—is issued in loose leaf to provide maximum flexibility. Ultimately the material comprising this identification manual on the German Navy will be as shown in the table of contents with such additional data as experimentation and experience prove to be of aid to the fighting forces. Meanwhile, to avoid delay in reaching the users of this and similar publications on foreign navies, introductory material and individual ship class jackets are issued as the information is processed and printed.

2. While the manual of each naval power is designed as a separate entity and bound in appropriate Naval War College colors for ready reference, the format is so arranged that the holders of these several manuals can make any special assembly which may be indicated by the operating area, the strategical or tactical situation obtaining, or the limitations of the unit upon which the user is embarked. To facilitate such assembly the forces afloat will be issued separate Task binders into which the interchangeable sheets may be arranged into air views only, target angles only or any combination suitable for a given theatre of operations.

3. ONI 204 is a "Restricted" publication. Subject to the limitations imposed by its classification, it is the intent that the responsible officer feel free to exercise such latitude and discretion in its circulation as to insure a familiarity on the part of the officers and men of our fighting forces, and those of other United Nations, with the units of the German Navy.

4. ONI 204 has been prepared from the best information available to the Navy Department. In the main, it is based upon published material and reconnaissance photographs. Except for fragmentary addenda which may be uncovered, the first source has been exhausted. It is expected that future revisions will derive largely from reconnaissance photographs and contributions (sketches and descriptions) from combat personnel.

5. Cases of mistaken identity resulting frequently in tragic consequences have occurred with disconcerting regularity among the European belligerents. These manuals are designed to facilitate timely recognition and to provide general and tactical information which may assist in the moment when contact with the enemy is first made.

6. Corrections and addenda to ONI 204 will be issued as information becomes available.

IN REPLY REFER TO INITIALS AND NO.

OP-16-F-20   SI/EF30

RESTRICTED   **SERIAL NO.** 3170216

/S/ H. C. TRAIN

CAPTAIN, U. S. NAVY

DIRECTOR OF NAVAL INTELLIGENCE

CHARACTERISTICS OF GERMAN NAVAL VESSELS

DIVISION OF NAVAL INTELLIGENCE—IDENTIFICATION AND CHARACTERISTICS SECTION —NOVEMBER, 1942

The larger and newer units of the German Navy resemble one another closely and share many common characteristics.

Their hulls show a marked sheer line, usually terminating in a characteristically snubbed clipper bow.

The low, rakish lines of the battleships and heavy cruisers have evolved through the higher and chunkier hulls of the older pocket battleships (now rated as heavy cruisers).

No two-stackers occur in the German Navy of a heavier classification than light cruisers. These ships stem from an older design type. Their stacks are rather slender, their sheer lines straighter, their hulls less rakish and they carry heavy tubular masts supporting light platforms.

The pre-Hitler battleships are unmistakable, with their low wide hulls and high stacks. Formerly three-stackers, the two forward funnels of these ships have been trunked

into a single heavy forward stack, and they now show two stacks of unequal thickness (see below).

German destroyers have low hulls, with long forecastles. They are two stackers, with flat-sided stacks of unequal thickness, topped by exceptionally high clinker-screens.

Torpedo boats and escort vessels are often one-stackers. Their hulls may be flush or broken and their stacks also show very high clinker-screens in most instances.

OLD BATTLESHIP   HEAVY CRUISER   BATTLESHIP

MINE SWEEPER   TORPEDO BOAT   DESTROYER   LIGHT CRUISER

German one stackers all have silhouettes that build up in pyramidal form to heavy tower foremasts. High aft rangefinders and bulbous A-A directors constitute unmistakable German elements in their design. "Humpbacked" main battery turrets characterize all new ships with the exception of Tirpitz.

Except in instances where masts have been applied to stacks, mainmasts are high, slender tripods or quadrupods.

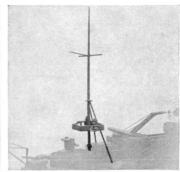

HEAVY TOWER FOREMASTS — SLENDER MAINMAST

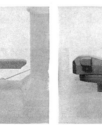

HIGH RANGE-FINDER — BULBOUS A-A DIRECTOR — SQUAT SINGLE STACKS

CRANE — SEARCH-LIGHT PLATFORMS — CATAPULT — HUMPBACKED TURRET

GERMAN ONE-STACKERS

DIVISION OF NAVAL INTELLIGENCE—IDENTIFICATION AND CHARACTERISTICS SECTION—SEPTEMBER, 1942

All the newer and more important ships of the German Navy are ONE-STACKERS. These ships are very similar in appearance, difficult to identify individually when seen in profile. It will be noted that aerial and bow or stern views are highly distinctive, however. The purpose of this chart is to call attention to the distinguishing characteristics of these ships.

GENERAL NOTES CAPITAL SHIPS:

Relatively low freeboard, wide beam, straight sides, considerable sheer forward of turrets, continuous hull curve stem to stern.

SCHARNHORST

Hangar abaft stack; tall tripod mainmast stepped well aft of stack just for'd of No. 3 turret.

PRINZ EUGEN
SEYDLITZ

Clipper bow, catapult against stack; tripod mainmast; searchlight cupolas on side of stack. Stack close to foremast.

ADMIRAL SCHEER

Clipper bow, pole foremast with wide bridge wings, prominent clinker screen to stack, heavy mainmast stepped just abaft stack.

NÜRNBERG

Raking bow, high bridge, built-in foremast. Stack with searchlight platform & mainmast catapult aft. Deck structure extending to high turret aft.

TIRPITZ

Pronounced gap in superstructure abaft stack; (noticeable from t.b. angles 45° to 135°) Centerline AA director cupolas abaft mainmast. Heavy pole mainmast. Searchlight cupolas on side of stack.

GNEISENAU

No hangar; tall mainmast stepped against trailing edge of stack; low stump mizzen aft.

ADMIRAL HIPPER

Raking stem, catapult against quadruped mainmast.

LÜTZOW

Plumb bow; stack well aft of foremast; pole foremast with large bridge; low clinker screen to stack; light mainmast abaft stack, catapult aft.

LEIPZIG

Clipper bow, low bridge, exposed pole foremast. Catapult for'd of stack. Heavy crane amidships.

Very wide beam. Wide box superstructure.

Beam considerably less than TIRPITZ. Narrow superstructure.

Narrow beam, flared hull sides. Bulky superstructure. Wide bridge & mast wings. Short masthead range-finder.

Narrow beam, flared hull sides. Tall masthead range finders. Pole foremast more noticeable in LÜT-ZOW.

NÜRNBERG   LEIPZIG

Narrow beam. Flared hull sides. Small mast-head range finders.

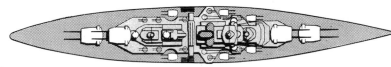

Wide hull with continuous curve stem to stern. Twin turrets. Large bridge. Three 5.9 gun broadside turrets.

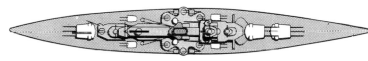

Continuous hull curve from stem to stern. Triple turrets. Cloverleaf boat deck amidships.

Narrow hull, flat amidships. Twin turrets. No broadside turrets.

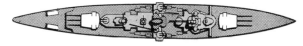

Continuous hull curve from stem to stern. Triple turrets prominent fore-&-aft. Shielded torpedo tubes on either quarter, aft.

Narrow hull; flat amidships. Break in deck at bridge, with deck house abreast of stack. Triple turrets, one for'd, 2 center-lined aft.

CAPITAL SHIPS—HEAVY

TIRPITZ:
Symmetrical profile. Easily mistaken for HIPPER-type cruiser except for large turrets, and wide beam.
TURRETS—
2-2 (twins). Very large. Flat crowns.

SCHARNHORST & GNEISENAU:
Relatively low freeboard; pronounced sheer to forecastle. Positions of turrets distinctive. GNEISENAU can be mistaken for ADMIRAL SCHEER.
TURRETS—
2-1 (triples). Large. Sloping crowns.

HEAVY CRUISERS

Higher freeboard, flared side to hull, tower fore-mast with small masthead range-finder-or-heavy pole foremast.

ADMIRAL HIPPER, PRINZ EUGEN, SEYDLITZ:
Symmetrical profile. Easily mistaken for TIRPITZ, except for small turrets, and tripod or quadruped mainmast. High turrets only have range finder hoods. All have same basic profile. Stack close to foremast tower, high curved cinder screen. Prominent AA director cupolas abreast of main-mast.
TURRETS—
2-2 (twins). Small. Low turrets flatter than high turrets.

ADMIRAL SCHEER, LÜTZOW:
Symmetrical profile. Single turrets fore-and-aft readily blend into superstructure. ADMIRAL SCHEER can be mistaken for GNEISENAU. Relatively high freeboard and less superstructure, low quarterdeck, heavy pole foremast.
TURRETS—
1-1 (triples). Large. Sloping crowns.

LIGHT CRUISERS

Broken deck with short forecastle, little sheer, pole foremast. Turrets—one forward, two aft.

NÜRNBERG & LEIPZIG:
"Pushed-forward" look to superstructure and super-firing turrets aft. NÜRNBERG especially resembles HIPPER class at bow angles.
TURRETS—
1-2 (triples). Small. Sloping crowns.

Jerry Jingles

Battleships

Ist dot nicht ein single-stack?
Ja, dot ist ein single-stack
(High in front, low in back)
Dot's a Jerry SINGLE-STACK!

Ist dot nicht ein tower-mast?
Ja, dot ist ein tower-mast
(Short und squat.   Learning fast!)
Dot's a Jerry TOWER-MAST!!

Tower-mast, single-stack,
Mast on funnel or in back
Load der guns and let her rip!
Dot's a Jerry BATTLESHIP!!!

Cruisers

Ist dot nicht ein battleship?
Nein, dot ain't no battleship.
Stack near foremast, easy seen
Dot's der HIPPER or EUGEN!

Ist dot nicht ein stein of beer?
Hell, dot ain't no stein of beer.
Turret forward, one in rear
LÜTZOW or der ADMIRAL SCHEER!

Ist dot nicht ein KREUZER craft?
Sure, dot ist ein KREUZER craft.
Turret forward, und two aft
NÜRNBERG—LEIPZIG KREUZER craft.

Ist dot nicht ein funny schmell?
Yah, das ist ein funny smell.
Schpindle mast, two stacks as well
Must be Jerry's old CL.

ONI 204

RESTRICTED

Timely identification in wartime may often mean the success or failure of an operation. Design similarities present a peculiar problem. This is strikingly illustrated in the case of the German navy, which insofar as its major units are concerned, may be termed a one-stacker navy. Attention is invited to the ONE-STACKER CHART. This page further develops cases of easily mistaken identity by illustrations of types which might easily be confused with the main German naval units by the untrained observer.

MISTAKEN IDENTITY

DIVISION OF NAVAL INTELLIGENCE—IDENTIFICATION AND CHARACTERISTICS SECTION—OCTOBER, 1942

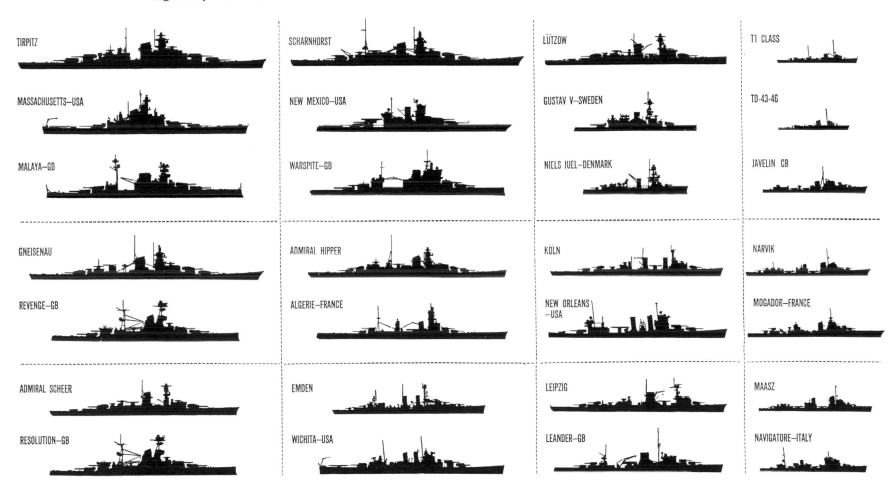

TIRPITZ

MASSACHUSETTS—USA

MALAYA—GB

SCHARNHORST

NEW MEXICO—USA

WARSPITE—GB

LÜTZOW

GUSTAV V—SWEDEN

NIELS IUEL—DENMARK

T1 CLASS

TD-43-4G

JAVELIN GB

GNEISENAU

REVENGE—GB

ADMIRAL HIPPER

ALGERIE—FRANCE

KÖLN

NEW ORLEANS —USA

NARVIK

MOGADOR—FRANCE

ADMIRAL SCHEER

RESOLUTION—GB

EMDEN

WICHITA—USA

LEIPZIG

LEANDER—GB

MAASZ

NAVIGATORE—ITALY

GERMAN CAMOUFLAGE

DIVISION OF NAVAL INTELLIGENCE—IDENTIFICATION AND CHARACTERISTICS SECTION—OCTOBER, 1942

NAVAL CAMOUFLAGE AS PRACTICED BY THE GERMANS HAS BEEN LIMITED ENTIRELY TO SURFACE DECEPTION AGAINST CLOSE–QUARTER ATTACK. IN EVERY CASE THE APPLICATION HAS BEEN MADE IN VIEW OF THE CONDITIONS UNDER WHICH THE SHIPS OPERATE—SHORT RANGE SWEEPS AND COASTAL SORTIES. THE VARYING TECHNIQUES ILLUSTRATED, REPRESENTING A FEW OF THE KNOWN CASES, ARE CONSIDERED AS A WHOLE ONLY PARTIALLY EFFECTIVE AND MERELY A CONTINUATION OF WORLD WAR I PRACTICE.

THE STRIPING ADOPTED FOR THE LARGER UNITS AND ILLUSTRATED HERE IS CONSIDERED ALMOST ENTIRELY USELESS. AT LONG RANGE THE COLORING BLENDS WITH THE SILHOUETTE, WHILE AT CLOSE RANGE THE CAMOUFLAGE IS NOT ADEQUATE FOR ANY TARGET DISTORTION.

↓ NÜRNBERG   PRINZ EUGEN ↑

GNEISENAU ↑

10°   30°   60°

90°   120°

GERMAN CAMOUFLAGE
DIVISION OF NAVAL INTELLIGENCE—IDENTIFICATION AND CHARACTERISTICS SECTION—OCTOBER, 1942

ADMIRAL HIPPER

THE TECHNIQUE APPLIED TO THE ADMIRAL HIPPER (TWO TOP STRIPS) WAS USED EARLIER IN THE WAR AND PRESUMABLY DROPPED. IT IS SHOWN HERE BECAUSE OF ITS SIMILARITY TO SOME BRITISH TECHNIQUES AND FOR WHATEVER TRAINING VALUE IT MAY HAVE.

THE DAZZLE PAINTING ILLUSTRATED BY THE MÖWE (TWO BOTTOM STRIPS) IS A GOOD APPLICATION FOR CLOSE RANGE TARGET DISTORTION. THE CONFUSION IS GAINED MAINLY FROM THE FALSE BEARING CREATED BY PAINTING CORNERS, STRIPING THE STACKS, ETC.

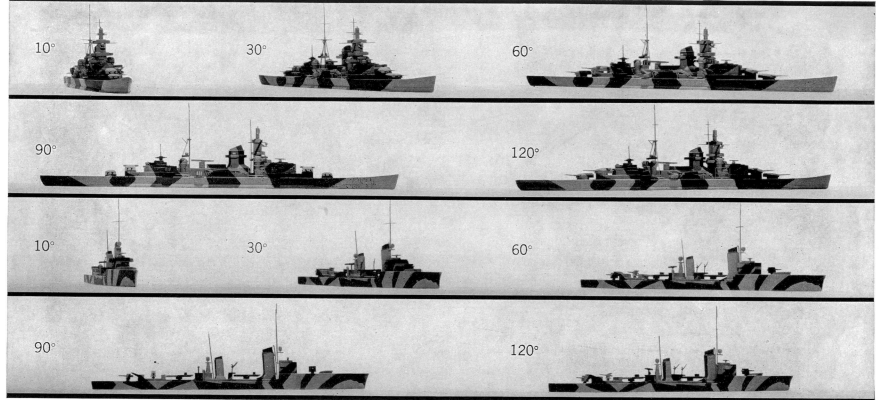

M-1

R CLASS

R CLASS

THE TECHNIQUE OF CAMOUFLAGE USED HERE IS TO CREATE A RANGE CONFUSION BY A THREE DIMENSIONAL DAZZLE. THE T-1 CLASS PHOTO SHOWS IT BY THE CUBES, INTENDED TO GIVE A PERSPECTIVE EFFECT. IN THE M-1 DRAWING THE

SAME EFFECT IS SOUGHT BY INTERTWINING TWO- OR THREE-COLOR PATTERNS.

THE SMALL-BOAT ZEBRA STRIPING FOLLOWS THE PLAN OF USING LARGE AREAS FOR DISTANCE CONFUSION, AND SMALL PATCHES FOR CLOSE

QUARTERS. ANOTHER STYLE IS ALSO SHOWN, WHICH IS ENTIRELY FUTILE, AS THE ENTIRE SILHOUETTE IS ACCENTUATED.

THE ZEBRA PAINTING IS CONSIDERED USEFUL ONLY IN SHORE-LINE OPERATIONS.

T-1

CONVERTED MOTOR-MINESWEEPER

⊕ GERMAN CAMOUFLAGE

DIVISION OF NAVAL INTELLIGENCE—IDENTIFICATION AND CHARACTERISTICS SECTION—OCTOBER, 1942

THE PATTERNS SHOWN ON THESE MISCELLANEOUS TRAWL-
ERS AND BARRAGE BREAKERS ILLUSTRATE PERHAPS THE
MOST SUCCESSFUL GERMAN CAMOUFLAGE. HOWEVER IT IS
ONLY A CONTINUATION OF WORLD WAR I PRACTICE AND
FAR BEHIND THE CURRENT U.S. AND BRITISH STANDARD.

↑ R BOAT

LIST OF GERMAN NAVAL VESSELS

B—BUILDING
?—STATUS DOUBTFUL
*—SUNK

BB-1	GNEISENAU	* DD-18	HANS LÜDEMANN	TB-43	ex-ODIN	XCM-1	COBRA	
BB-2	SCHARNHORST	* DD-19	HERMANN KUENNE	TB-44	ex-BALDER	XCM-2	KAISER	
* BB-3	BISMARCK	DD-20	KARL GALSTER	TB-45	ex-TOR	XCM-3	ROLAND	
BB-4	TIRPITZ	* DD-21	WILHELM HEIDKAMP	TB-46	ex-GYLLER	XCM-4	HANSASTADT	
? BB-5	"H"	* DD-22	ANTON SCHMIDT					
? BB-6	"I"	DD-23	Z-23	OTB-1	T-107	AM-1	M-60	
		DD-24	Z-24	OTB-2	T-108	AM-2	M-61	
OBB-1	SCHLESWIG-HOLSTEIN	DD-25	Z-25	OTB-3	T-110	AM-3	M-72	
OBB-2	SCHLESIEN	DD-26	Z-26	OTB-4	T-111	AM-4	M-75	
		DD-27	Z-27			AM-5	M-82	
CV-1	GRAF ZEPPELIN	DD-28	Z-28	B CD-1	NYMPHE (ex-TORDENSKJOLD)	AM-6	M-84	
? CV-2	"B"	DD-29	Z-29	B CD-2	THETIS (ex-HARALD HAAR-	AM-7	M-85	
		DD-30	Z-30		FAGRE)	AM-8	M-89	
CA-1	ADMIRAL HIPPER	DD-31	Z-31	B CD-3	ex-EIDSVOLD	AM-9	M-98	
* CA-2	BLÜCHER	DD-32	Z-32	B CD-4	ex-PEDER SKRAM	AM-10	M-102	
CA-3	PRINZ EUGEN	DD-33	Z-33	B CD-5	ex-HERTOG HENDRIK	AM-11	M-104	
B CA-4	SEYDLITZ	DD-34	Z-34	? CD-6	ex-LEMNOS	AM-12	M-109	
CA-5	ex-LÜTZOW (SOLD TO RUSSIA)	DD-35	Z-35	? CD-7	ex-KILKIS	AM-13	M-110	
CA-6	LÜTZOW	DD-36	Z-36	B CD-8		AM-14	M-111	
CA-7	ADMIRAL SCHEER	DD-37	Z-37			AM-15	M-115	
* CA-8	ADMIRAL GRAF SPEE	DD-38	Z-38	PG-1	F-1	AM-16	M-117	
		DD-39	Z-39	PG-2	F-2	AM-17	M-122	
CL-1	EMDEN	DD-40	Z-40	PG-3	KÖNIGIN LUISE	AM-18	M-126	
* CL-2	KÖNIGSBERG	DD 41	Z 41	PG-4	F-4	* AM 19	M-129	3IX OR MORE OTHERS
* CL-3	KARLSRUHE	DD-42	Z-42	PG-5	F-5			SUNK
CL-4	KÖLN	DD-43	Z-43	PG-6	HAI	AM-20	M-132	
CL-5	LEIPZIG	? DD-44	ex-WICHER	PG-7	F-7	AM-21	M-133	
CL-6	NÜRNBERG	? DD-45	ex-NORWEGIAN #1	PG-8	F-8	AM-22	M-134	
? CL-7	"M"	DD-46	ex-NORWEGIAN #2	PG-9	F-9	AM 23	M-136	
? CL 8	"N"	DD-47	ex-GERARD CALLENBURG	PG-10	F-10	AM-24	M-145	
? CL-9	"O"	DD-48	ex-TJERK HIDDES	PG-11	DRACHE	AM-25	M-146	
? CL-10	"P"	B DD-49	ex-LE FIER	PG 12	KLAUS VON BEVERN	* AM-26	M-157	
B CL-11	ex-ZEVEN PROVINZIEN	B DD-50	ex-L'AGILE	PG-13	T-196	AM-27-66	M-1-40—*SOME HAVE BEEN	
B CL-12	ex-EENDRACHT	B DD-51	ex-LE FAROUCHE	PG-14	METEOR			SUNK
		B DD-52	ex-L'ENTREPRENANT	PG-15	DELPHIN	AM-67	OXHOFT	
* DD-1	LEBERECHT MAASZ	B DD-53	ex-L'OPINIATRE	PG-16	FUCHS	AM-68	WESTERPLATTE	
* DD-2	GEORG THIELE	B DD-54	ex-L'AVENTURIER	PG-17	ELBE	AM-69	ex-SOLOVEN	
* DD-3	MAX SCHULTZ	? DD-55	ex-BASILEUS GIORGIOS I	PG-18	WESER	AM-70	ex-OTRA	
DD-4	RICHARD BEITZEN			PG-19	BRUMMER	? AM-71	ex-ROUMA	
DD 5	PAUL JACOBI	TB-1	MÖWE	* PG-20	BREMSE	? AM-72	ex-WILLEM VAN EWIJCK	
DD-6	THEODOR RIEDEL	* TB-2	ALBATROS	B PG-21		? AM-73	ex-PIETER FLORISZ	
DD-7	HERMANN SCHOEMANN	TB-3	GREIF	AVC—1	WESTFALEN	AM-74	ex-ABRAHAM VAN DER HULST	
* DD-8	BRUNO HEINEMANN	TB-4	SEEADLER	2	SCHWABENLAND			
* DD-9	WOLFGANG ZENKER	TB-5	FALKE	3	OSTMARK	AMc 1	R1-	
DD-10	HANS LODY	TB-6	KONDOR	4	FRIESENLAND	* PT-7-111	S-7-111	16 AND MORE SUNK,
* DD-11	BERND VON ARNIM	* TB-7	WOLF			(PLUS)	(PLUS)	INCLUDING NEW DE-
* DD-12	ERICH GIESE	TB-8	ILTIS	? CM-1	ex-GRYF			SIGN TYPE
* DD-13	ERICH KÖLLNER	TB-9	JAGUAR	CM-2	ALBATROS (ex-OLAV TRYGGVASON)			
DD-14	FRIEDRICH IHN	TB-10	LEOPARD	B CM-3	"A"			
DD-15	ERICH STEINBRINK	* TB-11	LUCHS	B CM-4	"B"			
DD-16	FRIEDRICH ECKOLDT	TB-12	TIGER	B CM-5	"C"			
* DD-17	DIETHER VON ROEDER	TB-13-42	T-1-30	B CM-6	"D"			

ONI 204 RESTRICTED

RANGE TABLE

DIVISION OF NAVAL INTELLIGENCE—IDENTIFICATION AND CHARACTERISTICS SECTION—SEPTEMBER, 1942

ESTIMATION OF RANGE BY OBSERVING THE AMOUNT OF SHIP SEEN ABOVE OR BELOW THE HORIZON.

EXPLANATION—TABLE OF DISTANCES OF SEA HORIZON.

THE DISTANCE CORRESPONDING TO THE POSITION AT WHICH THE HORIZON LINE CUTS THE SHIP PROFILE SHOULD BE FILLED IN FROM THE TABLE FOR THE OBSERVER AS FOLLOWS:

THE COLUMN "SHIP BEYOND THE HORIZON" SHOULD SHOW THE SUM OF THE DISTANCES OF THE SEA HORIZON (a) FOR HEIGHT OF EYE, (b) FOR HEIGHTS OF THE RESPECTIVE HORIZON LINES BEHIND THE PROFILE.

THE COLUMN "HORIZON BEYOND THE SHIP" SHOULD SHOW THE DIFFERENCE OF THESE TWO DISTANCES.

EXAMPLE—THE OBSERVER'S HEIGHT OF EYE IS 79 FEET. A SHIP IS SIGHTED BEYOND THE HORIZON WITH THE HORIZON LINE CUTTING ITS PROFILE AT A POINT 15 FEET ABOVE THE WATERLINE.

DISTANCE OF SEA HORIZON FOR 79′ = 20,610 YDS.
DISTANCE OF SEA HORIZON FOR 15′ = 8,980 YDS.
SUM = RANGE OF SHIP = 29,590 YDS.

HEIGHT IN FEET	DISTANCE OF SEA HORIZON	HEIGHT IN FEET	DISTANCE OF SEA HORIZON	HEIGHT IN FEET	DISTANCE OF SEA HORIZON	HEIGHT IN FEET	DISTANCE OF SEA HORIZON	HEIGHT IN FEET	DISTANCE OF SEA HORIZON	HEIGHT IN FEET	DISTANCE OF SEA HORIZON
1	2,320	21	10,630	41	14,840	61	18,110	81	20,870	101	23,300
2	3,280	22	10,880	42	15,020	62	18,260	82	20,990	102	23,420
3	4,020	23	11,120	43	15,200	63	18,400	83	21,120	103	23,530
4	4,640	24	11,360	44	15,380	64	18,550	84	21,250	104	23,640
5	5,190	25	11,590	45	15,550	65	18,690	85	21,380	105	23,760
6	5,680	26	11,820	46	15,720	66	18,840	86	21,500	106	23,870
7	6,140	27	12,050	47	15,890	67	18,980	87	21,630	107	23,980
8	6,560	28	12,270	48	16,060	68	19,120	88	21,750	108	24,090
9	6,960	29	12,490	49	16,230	69	19,260	89	21,870	109	24,200
10	7,330	30	12,700	50	16,400	70	19,400	90	21,990	110	24,320
11	7,690	31	12,910	51	16,560	71	19,540	91	22,120	111	24,430
12	8,030	32	13,120	52	16,720	72	19,670	92	22,240	112	24,540
13	8,360	33	13,320	53	16,880	73	19,810	93	22,360	113	24,650
14	8,680	34	13,520	54	17,040	74	19,940	94	22,480	114	24,750
15	8,980	35	13,720	55	17,200	75	20,080	95	22,600	115	24,860
16	9,280	36	13,910	56	17,350	76	20,210	96	22,720	116	24,970
17	9,560	37	14,100	57	17,500	77	20,340	97	22,830	117	25,080
18	9,840	38	14,290	58	17,660	78	20,480	98	22,950	118	25,180
19	10,110	39	14,480	59	17,810	79	20,610	99	23,070	119	25,290
20	10,370	40	14,670	60	17,960	80	20,740	100	23,180	120	25,400

HEIGHT OF OBSERVER

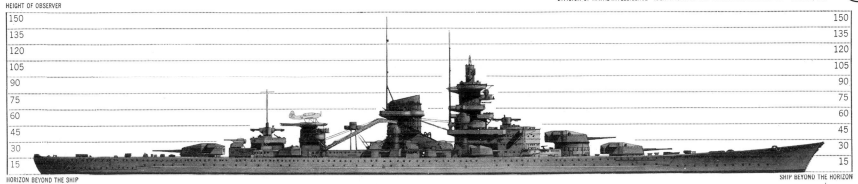

150		150
135		135
120		120
105		105
90		90
75		75
60		60
45		45
30		30
15		15

HORIZON BEYOND THE SHIP

SHIP BEYOND THE HORIZON

0

LENGTH 766' OA—741' WL
BEAM 98' 5"
DRAFT 24' 9" (MEAN)

DISPLACEMENT
26,000 TONS (STANDARD)

DENSITY OF FIRE
MAIN BATTERY

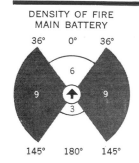

36°	0°	36°
	6	
9	↑	9
	3	
145°	180°	145°

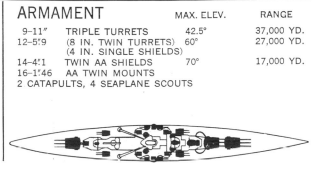

ARMAMENT

		MAX. ELEV.	RANGE
9—11"	TRIPLE TURRETS	42.5°	37,000 YD.
12—5".9	(8 IN. TWIN TURRETS)	60°	27,000 YD.
	(4 IN. SINGLE SHIELDS)		
14—4".1	TWIN AA SHIELDS	70°	17,000 YD.
16—1".46	AA TWIN MOUNTS		
2 CATAPULTS, 4 SEAPLANE SCOUTS			

PROTECTION

BELT—12" TO 13" AMIDSHIPS, 3" TO 4" ENDS
TURRETS—12"
BARBETTES—10"
F.C. TOWER—
SECONDARY BATTERY—2" (MAX) ON TURRETS AND BARBETTES
DECK—6"
UNDERWATER PROTECTION VERY COMPLETE

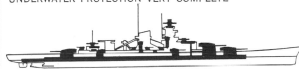

KNOTS	R.P.M.
	350
	300
30¼	275
	250
	245
27	240
	220
23	200
18	160
	150
12½	120
	80

DES. SPD DES. H.P.
30 KTS   80,000
29 KTS (TRIAL)

GNEISENAU—BB1

DIVISION OF NAVAL INTELLIGENCE—IDENTIFICATION AND CHARACTERISTICS SECTION—AUGUST, 1942

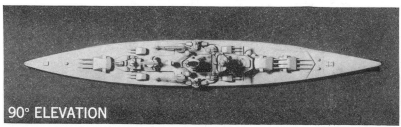

90° ELEVATION

PROFILE–2 TURRETS FOR'D
1 AFT
MAINMAST ON STACK
CATAPULT AFT
NO HANGAR
AERIAL–TRIPLE TURRETS
CLOVER LEAF ISLAND
AMIDSHIPS
END-ON—
NARROW BRIDGE
WIDE BEAM

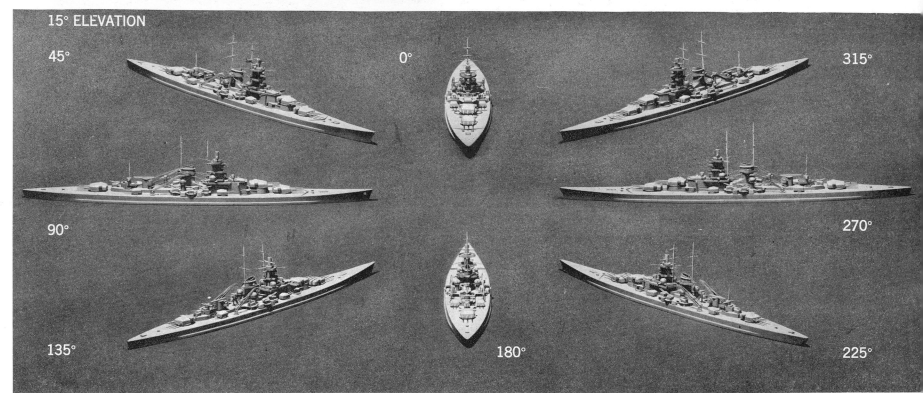

15° ELEVATION

45°

0°

315°

90°

270°

135°

180°

225°

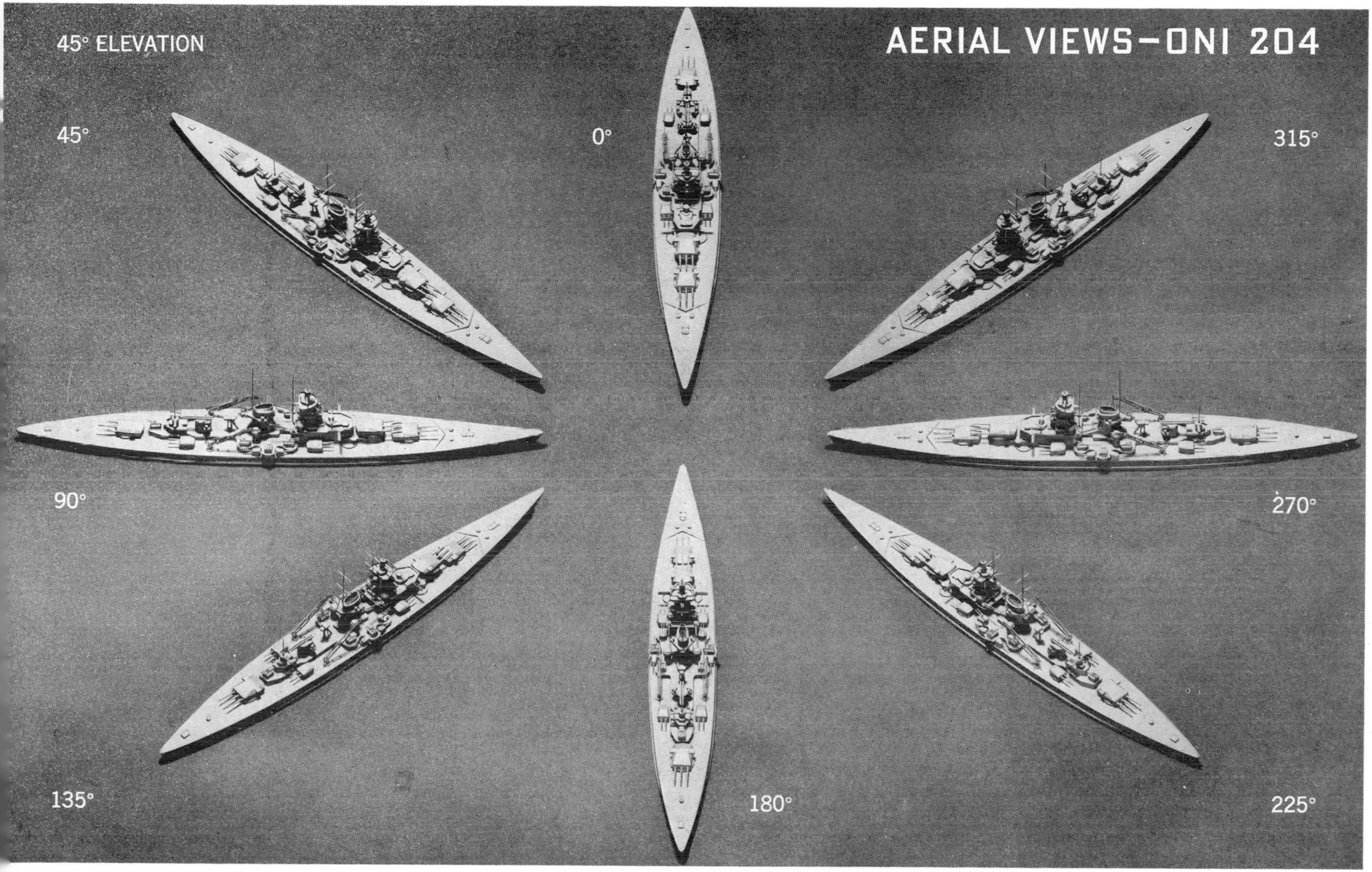

45°

0°

315°

90°

270°

135°

180°

225°

GNEISENAU—BB1 RESTRICTED

DIVISION OF NAVAL INTELLIGENCE—IDENTIFICATION AND CHARACTERISTICS SECTION—AUGUST, 1942

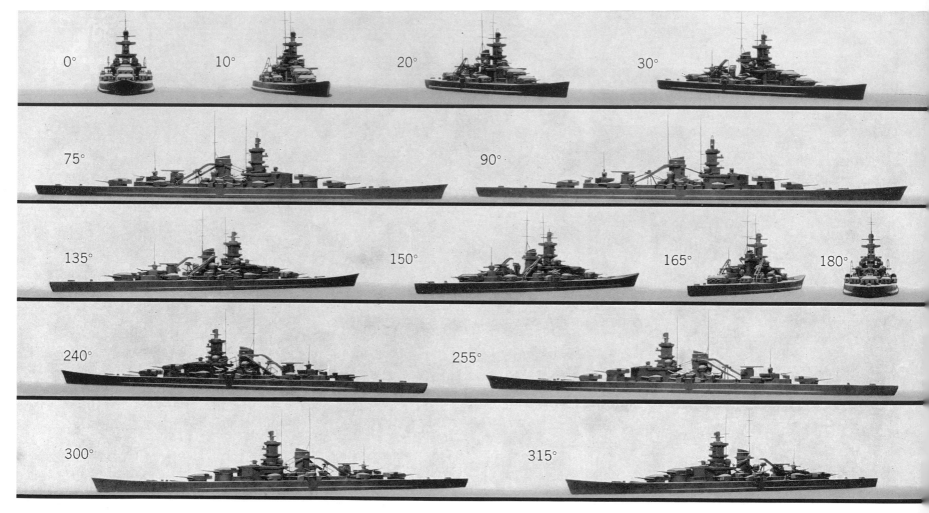

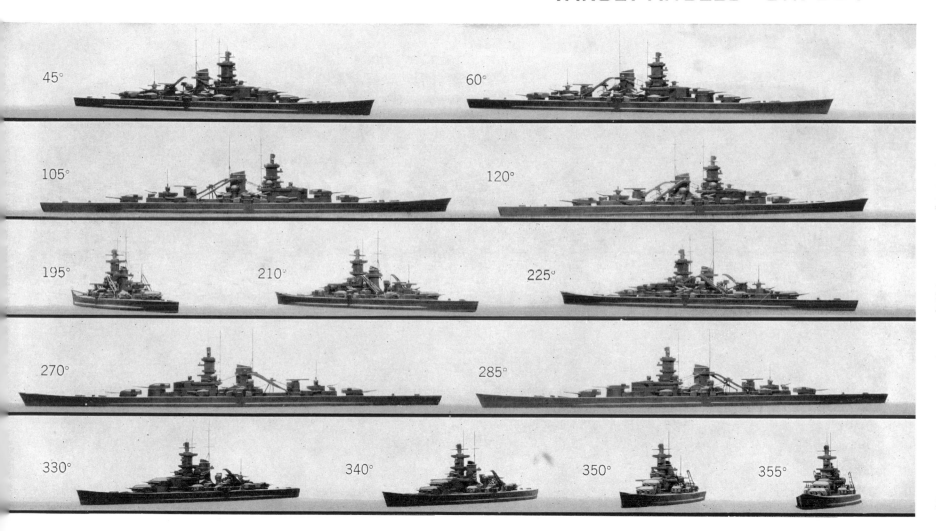

45° 60°

105° 120°

195° 210° 225°

270° 285°

330° 340° 350° 355°

GNEISENAU—BB1

DIVISION OF NAVAL INTELLIGENCE—IDENTIFICATION AND CHARACTERISTICS SECTION —AUGUST, 1942

BEGUN—FEBRUARY 14, 1934.   COMPLETED—MAY 21, 1938
SISTER SHIP—SCHARNHORST—BB2

ONI 204

RESTRICTED

1940–41

1940–41

CLINKER SCREEN HAS SINCE BEEN LOWERED AND FOREMAST RANGE FINDER ALTERED

1939

HEIGHT OF OBSERVER

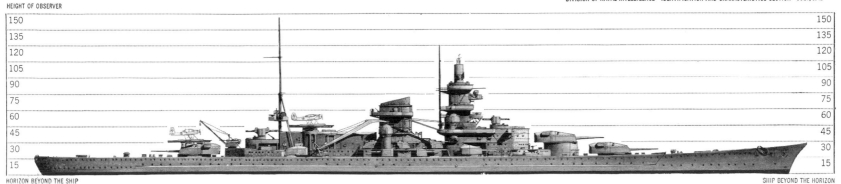

150	150
135	135
120	120
105	105
90	90
75	75
60	60
45	45
30	30
15	15

HORIZON BEYOND THE SHIP

SHIP BEYOND THE HORIZON

LENGTH 766' OA—741'-6" WL
BEAM   98'-5"
DRAFT 24'-7" (MEAN)

DISPLACEMENT
26,000 TONS (STANDARD)

DENSITY OF FIRE
MAIN BATTERY

36°	0°	36°
	6	
9	3	9
145°	180°	145°

ARMAMENT

	MAX. ELEV.	RANGE
9–11" TRIPLE TURRETS	42.5°	37,000 YD.
12–5".9 (8 IN TWIN TURRETS)	60°	27,000 YD.
(4 IN SINGLE SHIELDS)		
14–4".1 TWIN A.A. SHIELD	70° (SLANT)	17,000 YD.

16 PLUS SMALLER A.A.
2 CATAPULTS, 4 SEAPLANE SCOUTS

PROTECTION

BELT—12".6 MAIN—7".8 LOWER—(UNDER WATER)
TURRETS—14".3 FACE PLATES—10".6 SIDES—6".2 CROWNS
BARBETTES 10"
CONNING TOWER
SECONDARY BATTERY 2" (MAX.) ON TURRETS AND BARBETTES
DECKS—2" SECOND DECK 5".9 TO 4" THIRD DECK
THICKEST OVER VITALS.

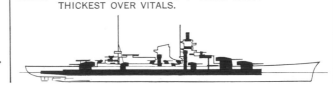

KNOTS	RPM
	350
	300
30¼	275
	250
	245
27	240
	220
23	200
18	160
	150
12½	120
	80

DES. SPD	DES. HP
28 KTS	80,000

SCHARNHORST—BB2

DIVISION OF NAVAL INTELLIGENCE—IDENTIFICATION AND CHARACTERISTICS SECTION—JULY, 1942

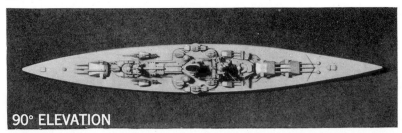

90° ELEVATION

PROFILE–TWO TURRETS FOR'D
1 AFT
MAINMAST ABAFT HANGAR

AERIAL–LONG HANGAR
CLOVER-LEAF ISLAND

END-ON–NARROW HIGH BRIDGE
WIDE BEAM

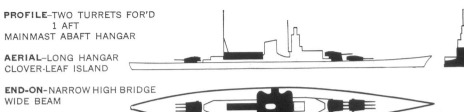

15° ELEVATION

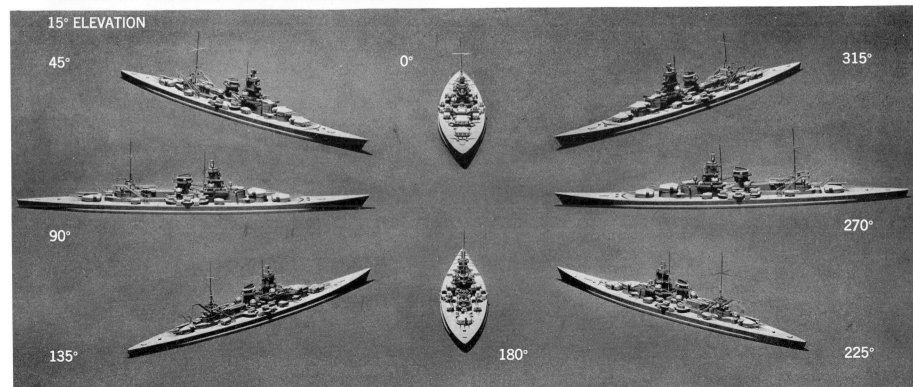

45°   0°   315°

90°   270°

135°   180°   225°

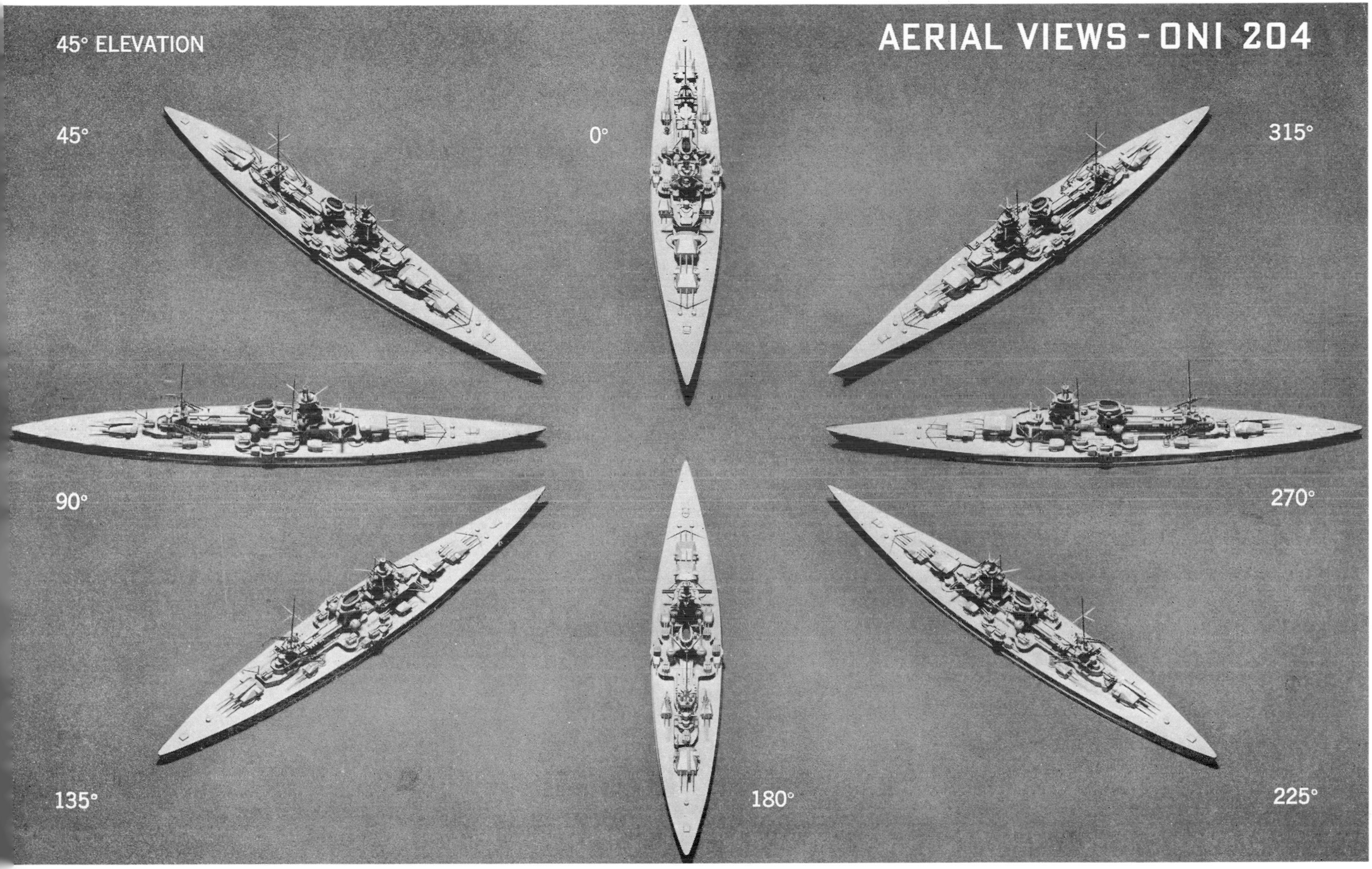

AERIAL VIEWS - ONI 204

45°

0°

315°

90°

270°

135°

180°

225°

SCHARNHORST—BB2 RESTRICTED

DIVISION OF NAVAL INTELLIGENCE—IDENTIFICATION AND CHARACTERISTICS SECTION—JULY, 1942

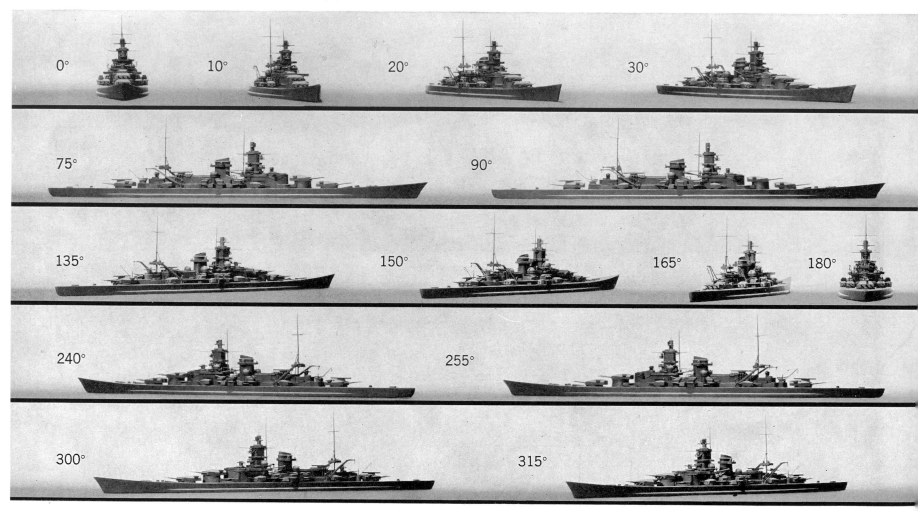

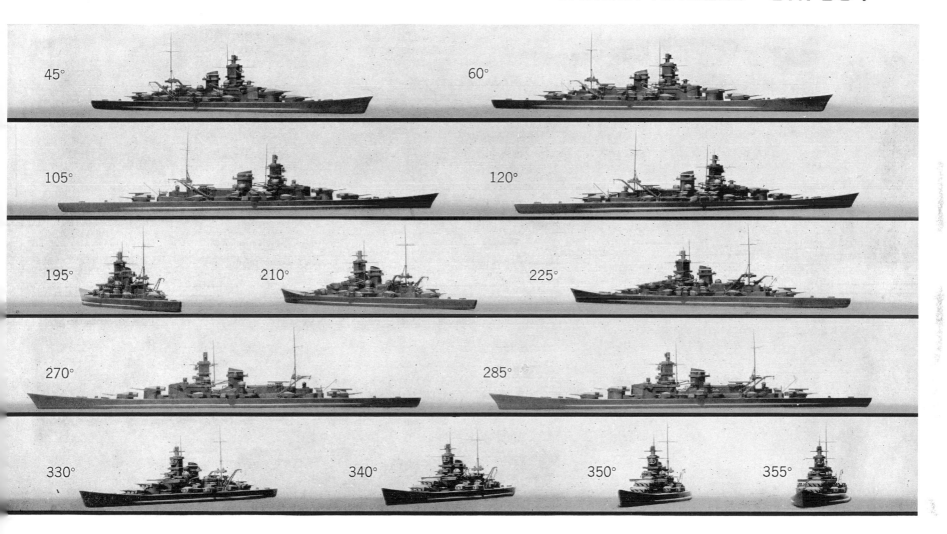

SCHARNHORST—BB2

DIVISION OF NAVAL INTELLIGENCE—IDENTIFICATION AND CHARACTERISTICS SECTION—JULY, 1942

BEGUN FEBRUARY 14, 1934. COMPLETED JANUARY 7, 1939
SISTER SHIP—GNEISENAU BB 1

ONI 204

RESTRICTED

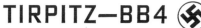
HEIGHT OF OBSERVER

150	150
135	135
120	120
105	105
90	90
75	75
60	60
45	45
30	30
15	15

HORIZON BEYOND THE SHIP

SHIP BEYOND THE HORIZON

0

LENGTH 817' OA—792'-4" WL
BEAM 118'-1"
DRAFT 33'-9" (MAX.)

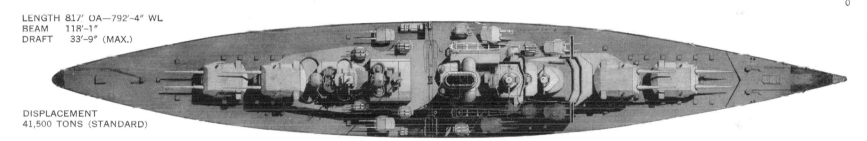

DISPLACEMENT
41,500 TONS (STANDARD)

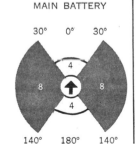

DENSITY OF FIRE
MAIN BATTERY

30°   0°   30°

4

8   ⬆   8

4

140°   180°   140°

ARMAMENT

		MAX. ELEV.	RANGE
8-15"	TWIN TURRET	40-45°	41,500 YD.
12-5".9	TWIN TURRET	45°	27,000 YD.
16-4".1	TWIN A.A. SHIELD	70°	17,000 YD.
		(SLANT)	YD.

40   SMALLER A.A.
6 21" TORPEDO TUBES (TRIPLES)
4 SEAPLANE SCOUTS 2 CATAPULTS (ATHWARTSHIPS)

PROTECTION

BELT—13" MAIN 5.7" UPPER
TURRETS—13.8" FACE PLATES 7.9" SIDES 6" CROWNS
CONNING TOWER 12.6"
BARBETTES 13.8"
SECONDARIES 2" (MAX.) ON TURRETS AND BARBETTES
DECKS 2" MAIN DECK 4.75"—3.2" THIRD DECK
THICKEST OVER VITALS

KNOTS	R.P.M.
	300
	275
	250
	245
31	240
30	220
	200
	160
	150
	120
	80

DES. SPD.   DES. H.P.
30¼ KTS   150,000

TIRPITZ—BB4

DIVISION OF NAVAL INTELLIGENCE—IDENTIFICATION AND CHARACTERISTICS SECTION—AUGUST, 1942

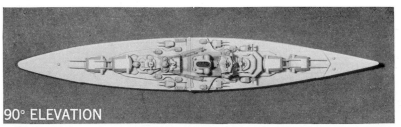

90° ELEVATION

PROFILE–2 TURRETS FOR'D
2 AFT
GAP AFT OF STACK

AERIAL–CONTINUOUS
HULL CURVE
3 BROADSIDE TURRETS

END ON–WIDE BEAM
HIGH WIDE BRIDGE

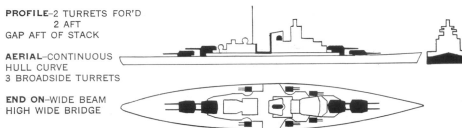

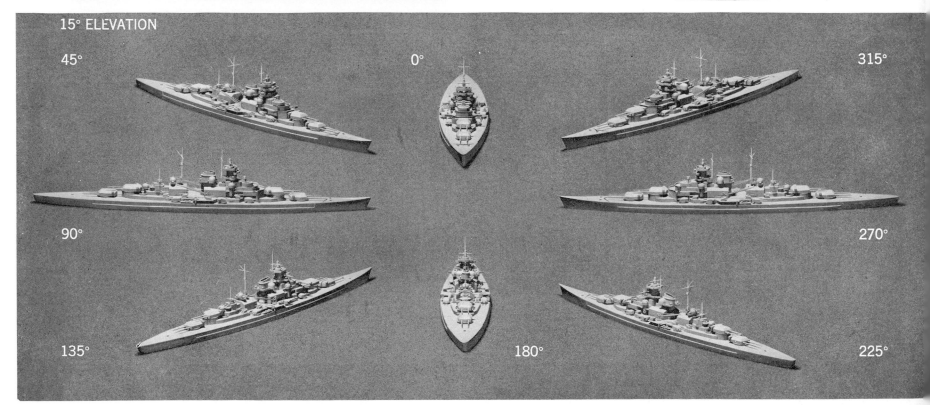

15° ELEVATION

45°

0°

315°

90°

270°

135°

180°

225°

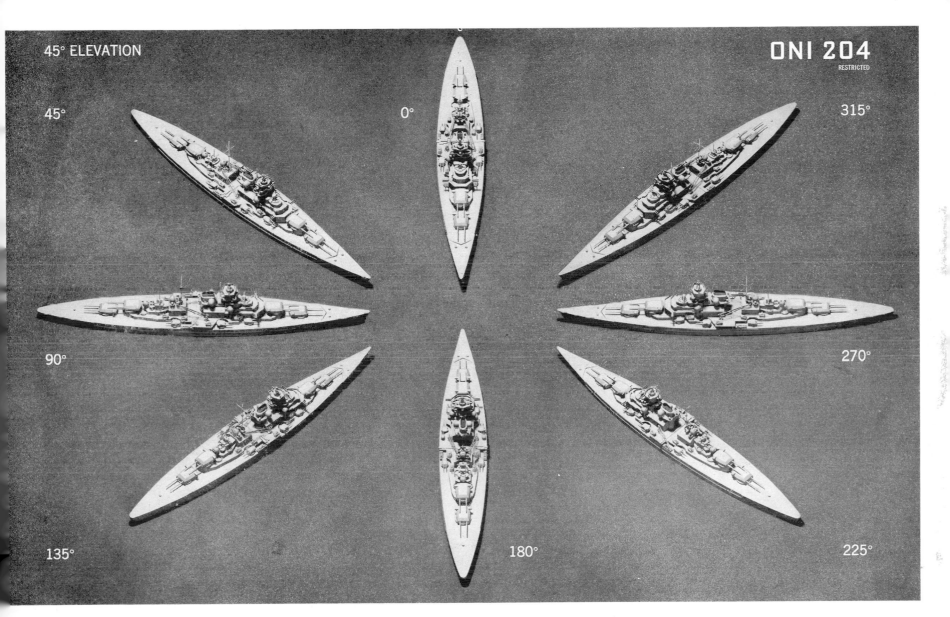

45°

0°

315°

90°

270°

135°

180°

225°

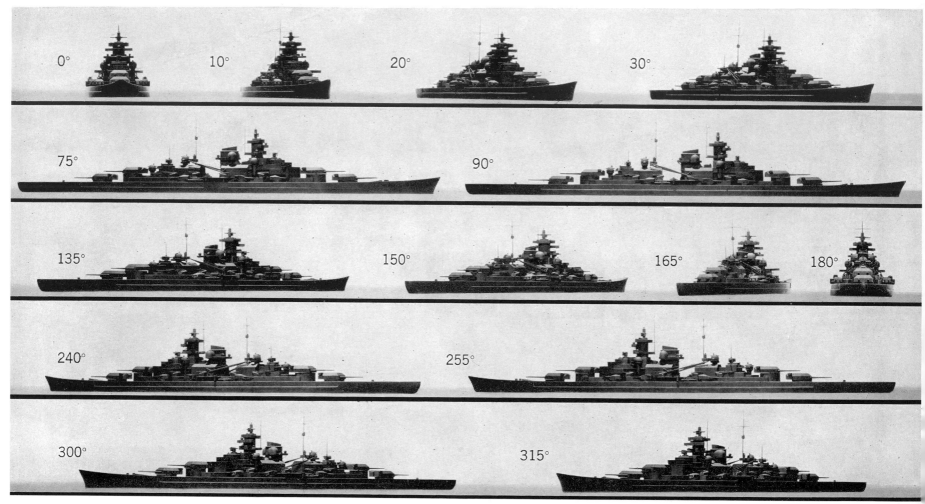

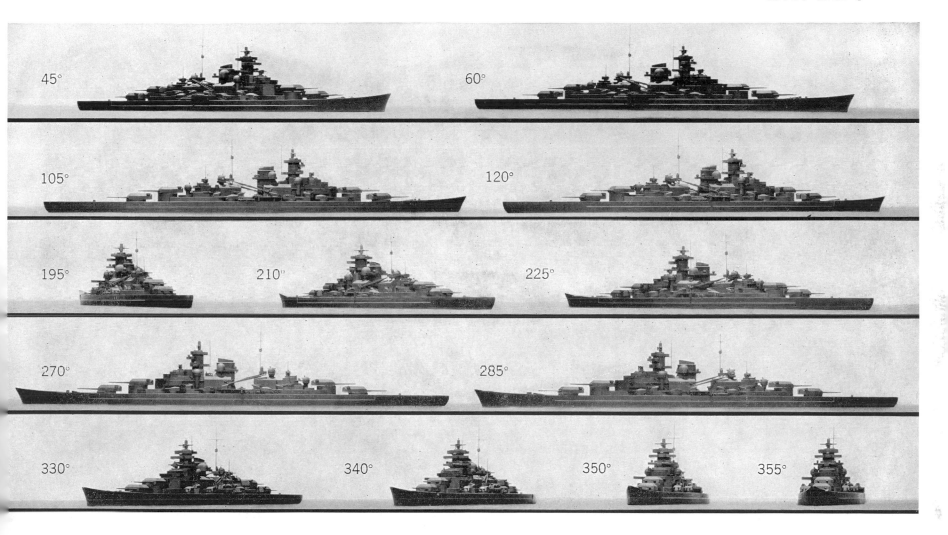

45°

60°

105°

120°

195°

210°

225°

270°

285°

330°

340°

350°

355°

TIRPITZ—BB4

DIVISION OF NAVAL INTELLIGENCE—IDENTIFICATION AND CHARACTERISTICS SECTION—AUGUST, 1942

BEGUN—OCTOBER 24, 1936. COMPLETED—NOVEMBER 10, 1940
SISTER SHIP—BISMARCK—SUNK MAY 27, 1941

ONI 204

RESTRICTED

ONI 204 RESTRICTED

BEGUN—1905. COMPLETED—1908
SISTER SHIP: SCHLESIEN—OBB1
CONVERTED INTO CADET TRAINING SHIPS—1936

SCHLESWIG-HOLSTEIN—OBB1

DIVISION OF NAVAL INTELLIGENCE—IDENTIFICATION AND CHARACTERISTICS SECTION —OCTOBER, 1942

ARMAMENT

	MAX. ELEV.	RANGE
4 –11″ TWIN TURRETS	30°	20,300
10–5″9 CASEMATES	21½°	16,600
4 –3″5 AA–SHIELDS	70°	13,700 (AT 39°)
4 –MG		

PROTECTION

BELT	—9½″ AMIDSHIPS; 4″ ENDS
TURRETS	—10″
BARBETTES	—11″
CONNING TOWER	—12″ FORE—6″ AFT
SECONDARY BATTERY	—6′ 9″
DECKS	—1½ TO 3″

UNDERWATER PROTECTION INADEQUATE
ACCORDING TO MODERN STANDARDS

PROPULSION

BOILERS	—12 SCHULTZ-THORNYCROFT "MARINE" TYPE
FUEL	—COAL AND OIL
DESIGNED HP	—17,000
DESIGNED SPEED	—18 KNOTS

LENGTH—419′ OA—413′ 1″ WL
BEAM —72′ 9″
DRAFT —25′ 3″ (MAXIMUM)

DISPLACEMENT—
12,300 TONS (STANDARD)

HEIGHT OF OBSERVER

HORIZON BEYOND THE SHIP

SHIP BEYOND THE HORIZON

SEIZURES-CD
DIVISION OF NAVAL INTELLIGENCE—IDENTIFICATION AND CHARACTERISTICS SECTION—SEPTEMBER, 1942

PROSPECTIVE EMPLOYMENT—GUARDSHIPS, CONVOY ESCORT
AMPHIBIAN OPERATION SUPPORT VESSEL

ONI 204
RESTRICTED

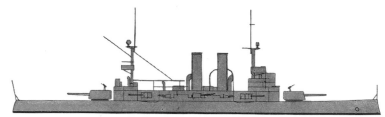

EIDSVOLD–CD 3 EX-NORWEGIAN

COMPLETED—1900 **SUNK**—BELIEVED RAISED BY GERMANS

DIMENSIONS—310'3" X 50'6" X 17'8" (MAXIMUM)

DISPLACEMENT—4,166 TONS (NORMAL)

ARMAMENT—2-8".2; 6-5".9; 8-3"

PROPULSION—HP 4,500 (DES.)

SPEED—16.5 KNOTS (DES.)   **ENDURANCE**—4,240 @ 10 KNOTS

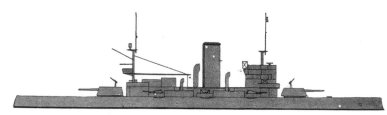

NYMPHE (EX-TORDENSKJOLD)–CD 1
THETIS (EX-HARALD HAARFAGRE)–CD 2 EX-NORWEGIAN

COMPLETED—1897
REPORTED RE-FITTED AND RE-ARMED IN GERMANY

DIMENSIONS—304' X 48'6" X 17'8" (MAXIMUM)

DISPLACEMENT—3,858 TONS (NORMAL)

ARMAMENT—2-8".2; 6-4".7; 6-3"; 2-3" AA

PROPULSION—HP 4,500 (DES.)

SPEED—16.5 KNOTS (DES.)   **ENDURANCE**—4,720 @ 10 KNOTS

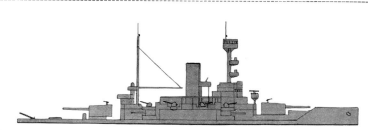

PEDER SKRAM–CD 4 EX-DANISH

COMPLETED—1908

DIMENSIONS—286'7" X 51'6" X 16'4" (MAXIMUM)

DISPLACEMENT—3,500 TONS (STANDARD)

ARMAMENT—2-9".4; 4-5".9; 8-3"; 2-1".45 **TORPEDO TUBES, 4-18"**

PROPULSION—HP 5,400

SPEED—16 KNOTS (DES.)   **ENDURANCE**—1,940 @ 10 KNOTS

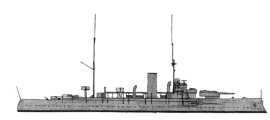

HERTOG HENDRIK–CD 5 EX-DUTCH

COMPLETED—JANUARY 5, 1904 **TRAINING SHIP**
DIMENSIONS—316'11" X 49'10" X 19'1" (MAXIMUM)
DISPLACEMENT—5,000 TONS (NORMAL)
ARMAMENT—1-9".45; 4-5".9; 2-3"; 2-1".57; 4-1".46
PROPULSION—HP 6,400 (DES.)
SPEED—16 KNOTS (DES.)   **ENDURANCE**—4,100 @ 9.2 KNOTS

LEMNOS (EX-IDAHO)–CD 6, KILKIS (EX-MISSISSIPPI)–CD 7, EX-GREEK
BELIEVED BEING RAISED BY GERMANS

HEIGHT OF OBSERVER

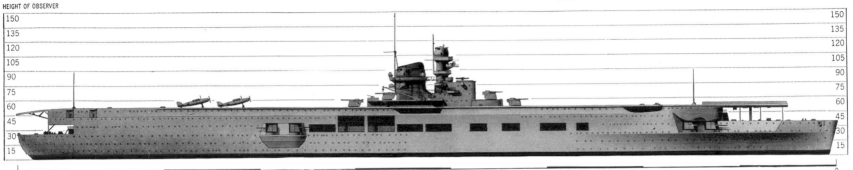

150	150
135	135
120	120
105	105
90	90
75	75
60	60
45	45
30	30
15	15
	0

HORIZON BEYOND THE SHIP

SHIP BEYOND THE HORIZON

LENGTH—820' WL 850' OA (EST)
BEAM —88'-7"
DRAFT —18'-4"

DISPLACEMENT—19,000 TONS

ARMAMENT

16–5".9
10–4".1

18–1".46 AA
4–0".79 AA

AIRCRAFT–40 (OFFICIAL)

PROTECTION

BELT—2-⅓"
CASEMATES FOR 5".9 GUNS

PROPULSION

HP —110,000
SPEED—32 KNOTS

IT IS KNOWN THAT CERTAIN SUPERSTRUCTURAL FEATURES, INCLUDING AA BATTERY DISPOSITION, VARY FROM THESE DRAWINGS, WHICH ARE BELIEVED SUBSTANTIALLY CORRECT FOR HULL PROPORTION AND GENERAL OUTLINE. DETAILS OF PROFILES, AIR VIEWS AND TARGET ANGLES AWAIT BETTER RECONNAISSANCE PHOTOGRAPHS.

GRAF ZEPPELIN—CV1
DIVISION OF NAVAL INTELLIGENCE—IDENTIFICATION AND CHARACTERISTICS SECTION—SEPTEMBER, 1942

BEGUN—DECEMBER 1, 1936
DATA ON GERMAN CARRIERS IS LACKING IN SEVERAL IMPORTANT
DETAILS, INCLUDING COMPLETION DATE OF GRAF ZEPPELIN.

ONI 204
RESTRICTED

R.A.F., 1941 ↓   DECEMBER 8, 1938 ↑

HEIGHT OF OBSERVER

150	150
135	135
120	120
105	105
90	90
75	75
60	60
45	45
30	30
15	15

HORIZON BEYOND THE SHIP

SHIP BEYOND THE HORIZON

0

LENGTH 655' OA—639'-9" WL
BEAM 69'-11"
DRAFT 15'-5" (MEAN)

DISPLACEMENT
10,000 TONS (STANDARD)

DENSITY OF FIRE MAIN BATTERY

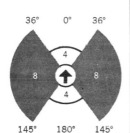

36°	0°	36°
4		
8	↑	8
4		
145°	180°	145°

ARMAMENT

	MAX. ELEV.	RANGE
8–8" TWIN TURRETS	70°	17,000 YD.
12–4".1 (D.P.)	(SLANT)	

12 (PLUS) A.A.
12–21" TORPEDO TUBES (TRIPLES)
1 CATAPULT, 3 SEAPLANE SCOUTS

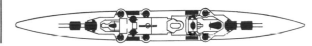

PROTECTION

BELT—4" ESTIMATED
TURRETS
CONNING TOWER—2"
RANGEFINDERS—2"
DECKS—THIRD DECK—3¼"

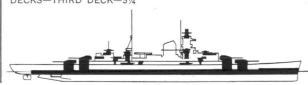

KNOTS	RPM
	420
	400
	350
	300
	275
	250
	245
	240
	220
	200
	160
	150
	120
	80

DES. SPD	DES. HP
32 KTS	95,000

ADMIRAL HIPPER—CA1

DIVISION OF NAVAL INTELLIGENCE—IDENTIFICATION AND CHARACTERISTICS SECTION—JULY, 1942

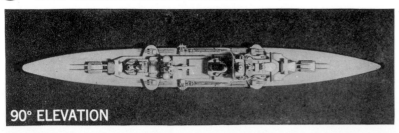

90° ELEVATION

PROFILE–RAKING STEM
CATAPULT AGAINST
QUADRUPOD MAINMAST

AERIAL–NARROW HULL,
FLAT AMIDSHIPS
TWIN TURRETS,
TWO FORWARD—TWO AFT

END-ON–
NARROW BEAM
WIDE BRIDGE AND
MAST WINGS

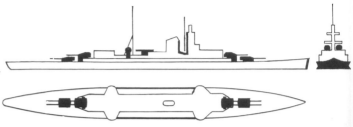

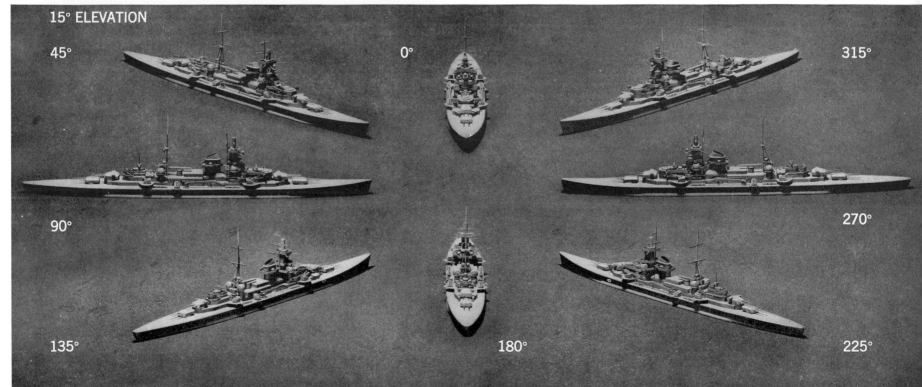

15° ELEVATION

45°

0°

315°

90°

270°

135°

180°

225°

45°

0°

315°

90°

270°

135°

180°

225°

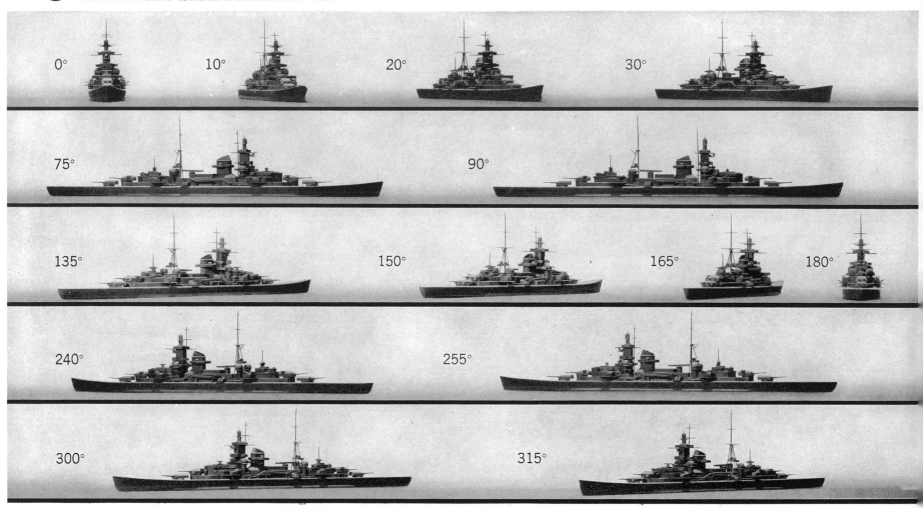

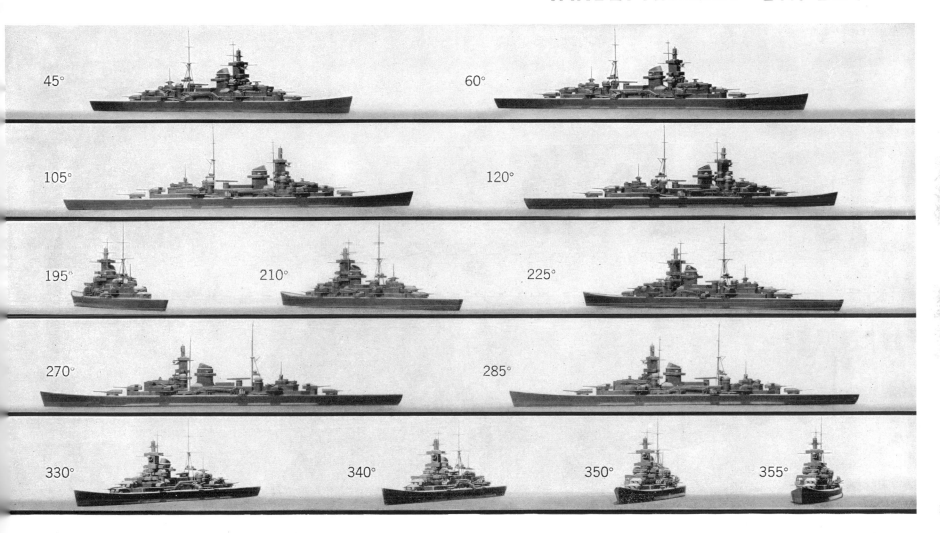

ADMIRAL HIPPER—CA1

DIVISION OF NAVAL INTELLIGENCE—IDENTIFICATION AND CHARACTERISTICS SECTION—JULY, 1942

BEGUN—JAN. 18, 1935   COMPLETED—APR. 29, 1939
SISTER SHIPS—EUGEN, SEYDLITZ, EX-LÜTZOW (SOLD TO RUSSIA)
BLÜCHER (SUNK APRIL 9, 1940)

ONI 204

RESTRICTED

R.A.F. JAN. 26, 1941

HORIZON BEYOND THE SHIP

SHIP BEYOND THE HORIZON

LENGTH 682' OA—654'-6" WL
BEAM 71' 2"
DRAFT 15'-6" (MEAN)

DISPLACEMENT
10,000 TONS (STANDARD)

DENSITY OF FIRE MAIN BATTERY

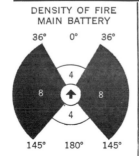

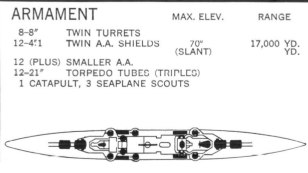

ARMAMENT

		MAX. ELEV.	RANGE
8-8"	TWIN TURRETS		
12-4"1	TWIN A.A. SHIELDS	70° (SLANT)	17,000 YD. YD.
12 (PLUS) SMALLER A.A.			
12-21"	TORPEDO TUBES (TRIPLES)		
1 CATAPULT, 3 SEAPLANE SCOUTS			

PROTECTION

BELT—4"—5" (EST.)
TURRETS—
BARBETTES—
CONNING TOWER—RF 2"
DECKS—THIRD DECK—3¼"

KNOTS	R.P.M
	420
	400
	350
	300
	275
	245
	240
	220
	200
	160
	150
	120
	80

DES. SPD	DES. H.P.
32 KTS	95,000

PRINZ EUGEN—CA3

DIVISION OF NAVAL INTELLIGENCE—IDENTIFICATION AND CHARACTERISTICS SECTION—AUGUST, 1942

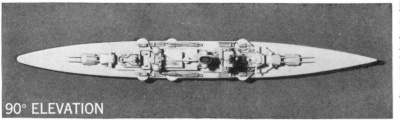

90° ELEVATION

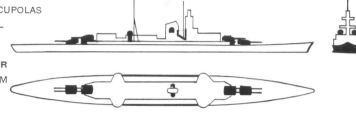

PROFILE-CLIPPER BOW
TRIPOD MAINMAST.
STACK SEARCHLIGHT CUPOLAS

AERIAL-NARROW HULL
FLAT AMIDSHIPS
TWIN TURRETS—
TWO FOR'D—TWO AFT
CATAPULT—HANGAR
REVERSE FROM **HIPPER**

END-ON-NARROW BEAM
WIDE BRIDGE-AND
MAST-WINGS

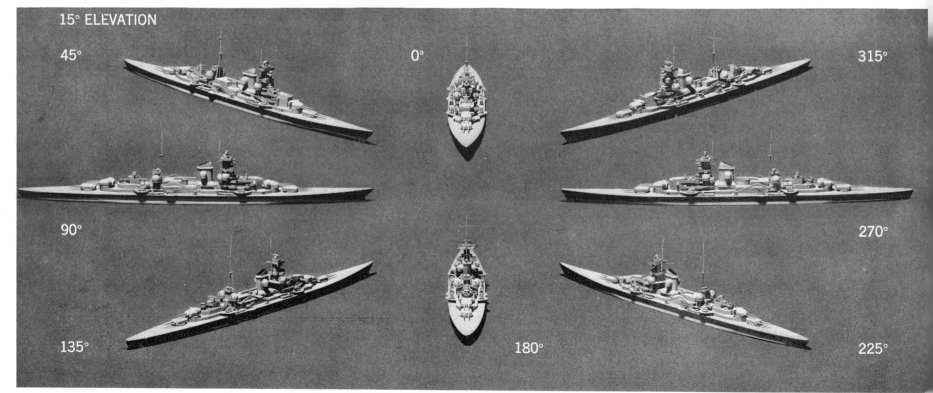

15° ELEVATION

45° 0° 315°

90° 270°

135° 180° 225°

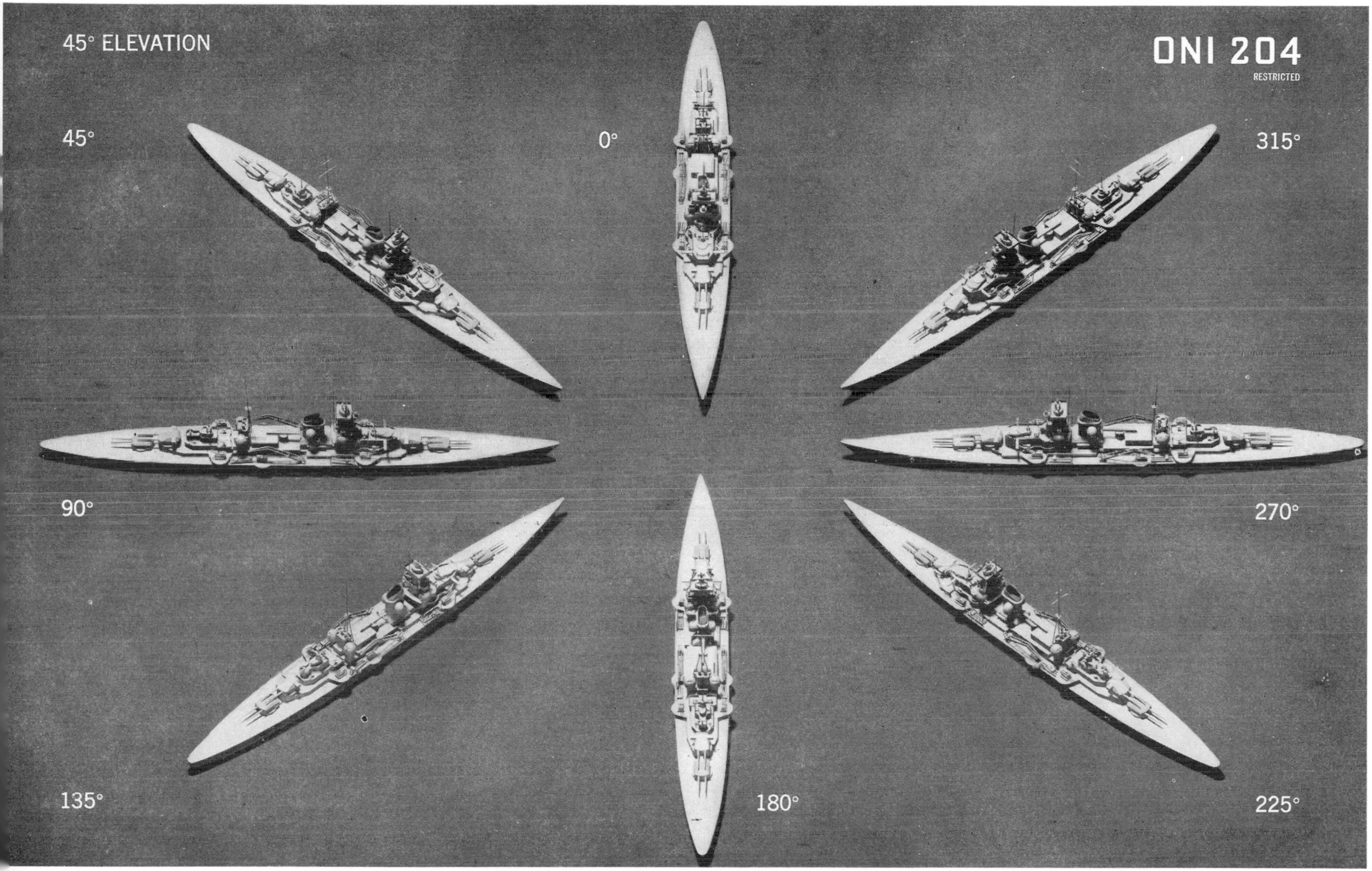

45°

0°

315°

90°

270°

135°

180°

225°

PRINZ EUGEN—CA3

DIVISION OF NAVAL INTELLIGENCE—IDENTIFICATION AND CHARACTERISTICS SECTION—AUGUST, 1942

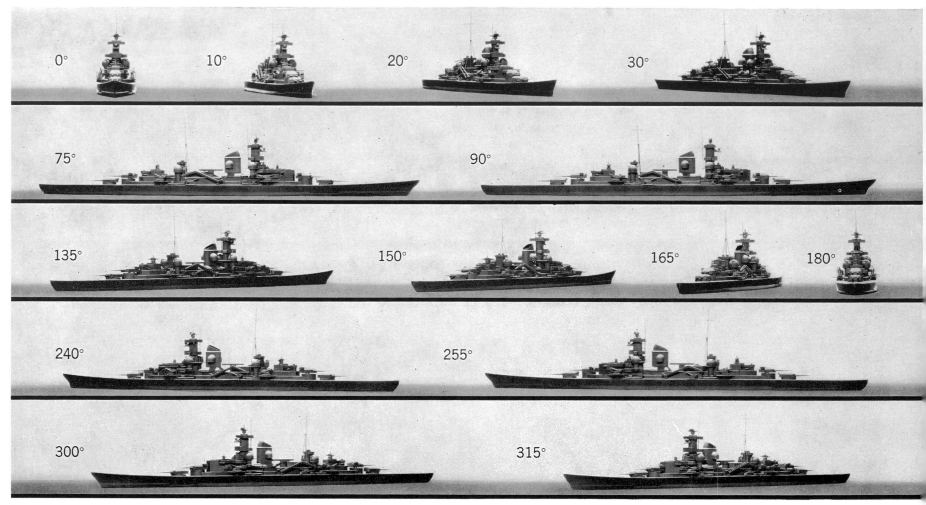

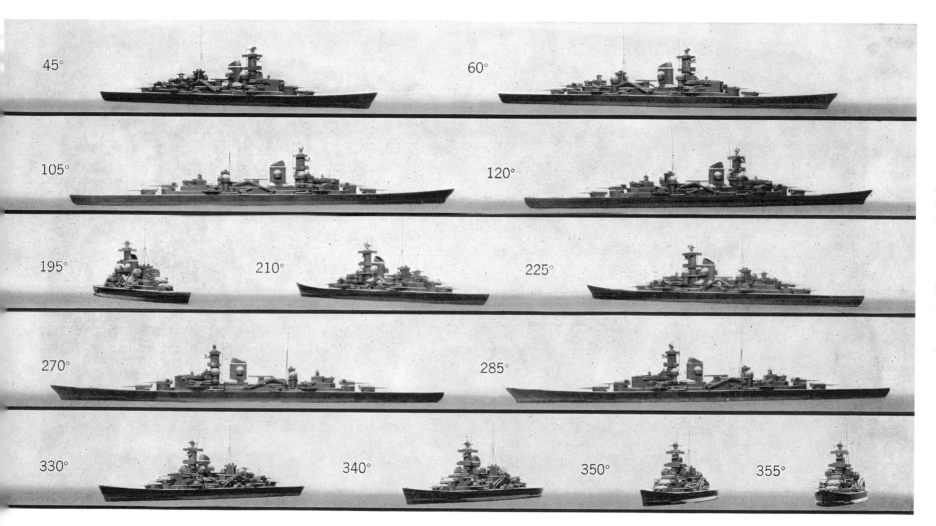

45°

60°

105°

120°

195°   210°   225°

270°   285°

330°   340°   350°   355°

PRINZ EUGEN—CA3

DIVISION OF NAVAL INTELLIGENCE—IDENTIFICATION AND CHARACTERISTICS SECTION—AUGUST, 1942

BEGUN–APRIL 1, 1936. COMPLETED–APRIL, 1940
SISTER SHIPS HIPPER (CA1)—SEYDLITZ (CA4), COMPLETING
EX-LUETZOW, TURNED OVER TO RUSSIA

ONI 204

R.A.F. MAY 17, 1942

30' STERN MISSING BY TORPEDOING

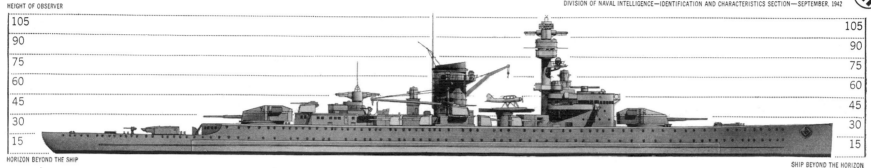

HORIZON BEYOND THE SHIP

SHIP BEYOND THE HORIZON

LENGTH—609'-3" OA—596'-2" WL
BEAM —68'-3"
DRAFT —23'-3" (MAXIMUM)
       16'-5" (MEAN)

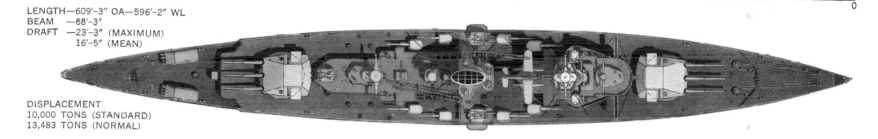

DISPLACEMENT
10,000 TONS (STANDARD)
13,483 TONS (NORMAL)

DENSITY OF FIRE MAIN BATTERY

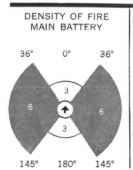

ARMAMENT

		MAX. ELEV.	RANGE
6–11"	50 CAL.	40°	36,000 YDS.
8–5".9	50 CAL.	30-40°	27,000 YDS.
6–4".1	AA TWIN MOUNTS	85°	
8–1".46	AA TWIN MOUNTS		
8–21"	TORPEDO TUBES (QUADRUPLE)		
AIRCRAFT—2 FLOAT PLANES;			
1 CATAPULT			

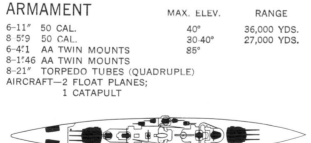

PROTECTION

BELT—   4" WITH 1½" INTERNALLY
TURRETS—   4"   BASES
                   5½" FACES
                   2-3" SIDES
CONNING TOWER—5"   DECKS—1½"—2½"
                   2" ROOF   3" OVER VITALS
UNDERWATER PROTECTION VERY COMPLETE
EXTERNAL BULGES

KNOTS	R.P.M.
	420
	400
	350
	300
	275
	250
	245
	240
	220
25	200
20	160
	150
15	120
10	80

DES. SPD. DES. H.P.
28 KTS.   54,000

LÜTZOW—CA6

DIVISION OF NAVAL INTELLIGENCE—IDENTIFICATION AND CHARACTERISTICS SECTION—SEPTEMBER, 1942

90° ELEVATION

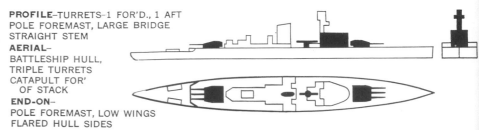

PROFILE—TURRETS–1 FOR'D., 1 AFT
POLE FOREMAST, LARGE BRIDGE
STRAIGHT STEM
AERIAL—
BATTLESHIP HULL,
TRIPLE TURRETS
CATAPULT FOR'
OF STACK
END-ON—
POLE FOREMAST, LOW WINGS
FLARED HULL SIDES

15° ELEVATION

45°   0°   315°

90°   270°

135°   180°   225°

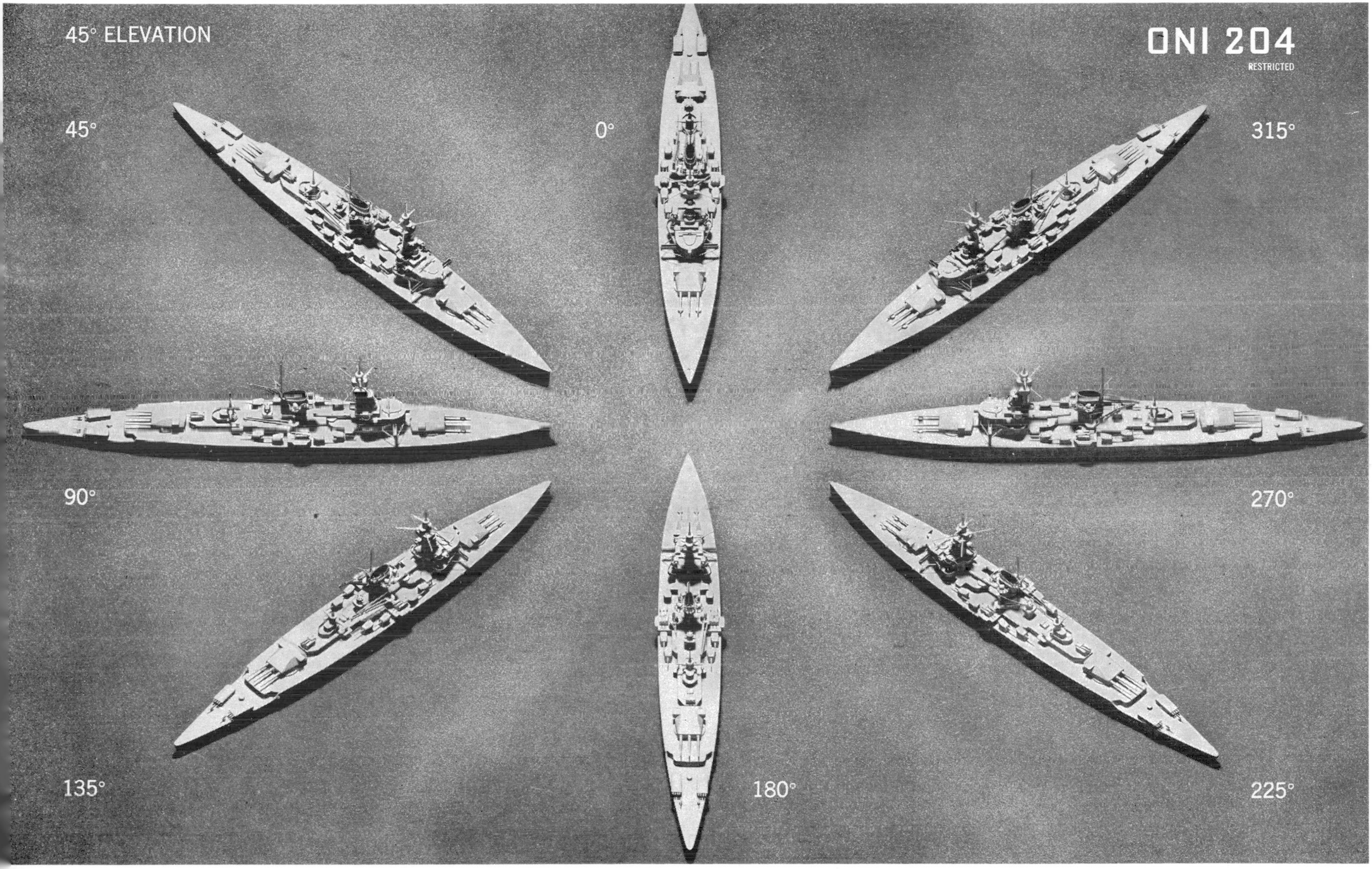

45°

0°

315°

90°

270°

135°

180°

225°

LÜTZOW—CA6

DIVISION OF NAVAL INTELLIGENCE—IDENTIFICATION AND CHARACTERISTICS SECTION —SEPTEMBER, 1942

0°   10°   20°   30°

75°   90°

135°   150°   165°   180°

240°   255°

300°   315°

45°

60°

105°

120°

195°

210°

225°

270°

285°

330°

340°

350°

355°

LÜTZOW—CA6
DIVISION OF NAVAL INTELLIGENCE—IDENTIFICATION AND CHARACTERISTICS SECTION—SEPTEMBER, 1942

BEGUN—MAY 2, 1929.   COMPLETED—JAN. 4, 1933
SISTER SHIPS: ADMIRAL SCHEER—CA7
ADMIRAL GRAF SPEE—SUNK DECEMBER 17, 1939

ONI 204
RESTRICTED

1937 ↑   1937 ↓   1939–40 ↑

HEIGHT OF OBSERVER

120	120
105	105
90	90
75	75
60	60
45	45
30	30
15	15

HORIZON BEYOND THE SHIP

SHIP BEYOND THE HORIZON

0

LENGTH—617' 8" OA—596' 2" WL
BEAM   —71' 1"
DRAFT —19' 8" MAX—16' 5" (MEAN)

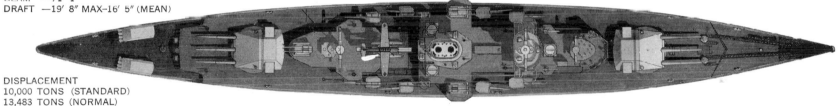

DISPLACEMENT
10,000 TONS (STANDARD)
13,483 TONS (NORMAL)

DENSITY OF FIRE MAIN BATTERY

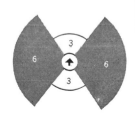

ARMAMENT

	MAX. ELEV.	RANGE
6–11" (50) TRIPLE TURRETS	40°	36,100 YD.
8–5".9 (50) TWIN	30–40°	27,000 YD.
6–4".1 AA TWIN	85°	
8–1".46 AA TWIN		
TORPEDOES 8–21"		
AIRCRAFT—2 FLOAT PLANES, 1 CATAPULT		

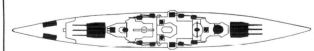

PROTECTION

BELT—4" AMIDSHIPS TAPERING TO 2" FORWARD AND AFT
TURRETS—7" FACE PLATE—2" SIDES—5" TO 3" TOP
BARBETTES—4"
CONNING TOWER—5" WITH 3" TOP
DECKS—1" MAIN DECK; 1½" SECOND DECK, 3" OVER VITALS
UNDERWATER PROTECTION VERY COMPLETE;
EXTERNAL BULGES

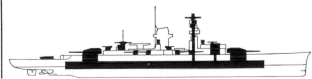

KNOTS	R.P.M.
	420
	400
	350
	300
	275
	250
	245
	240
	220
25	200
20	160
	150
15	120
10	80

DES SPD	DES HP
28 KTS	54,000

ADMIRAL SCHEER—CA 7

DIVISION OF NAVAL INTELLIGENCE—IDENTIFICATION AND CHARACTERISTICS SECTION—SEPTEMBER, 1942

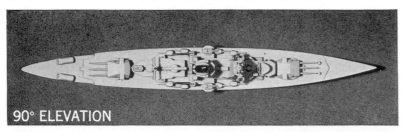

90° ELEVATION

PROFILE—TURRETS—1 FOR'D, 1 AFT
POLE FOREMAST
LOW BRIDGE
CLIPPER BOW

AERIAL—BATTLESHIP
HULL, BROKEN AFT
TRIPLE TURRETS
CATAPULT ABAFT STACK

END-ON—POLE FOREMAST,
WIDE WINGS, FLARED HULL SIDES

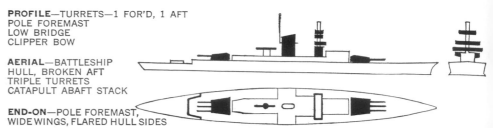

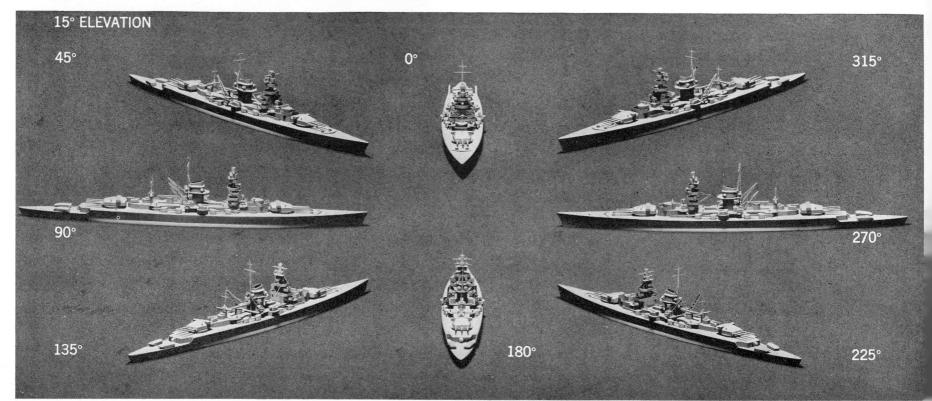

15° ELEVATION

45° 0° 315°

90° 270°

135° 180° 225°

45° ELEVATION

ONI 204
RESTRICTED

45°

0°

315°

90°

270°

135°

180°

225°

ADMIRAL SCHEER—CA 7

DIVISION OF NAVAL INTELLIGENCE—IDENTIFICATION AND CHARACTERISTICS SECTION—SEPTEMBER, 1942

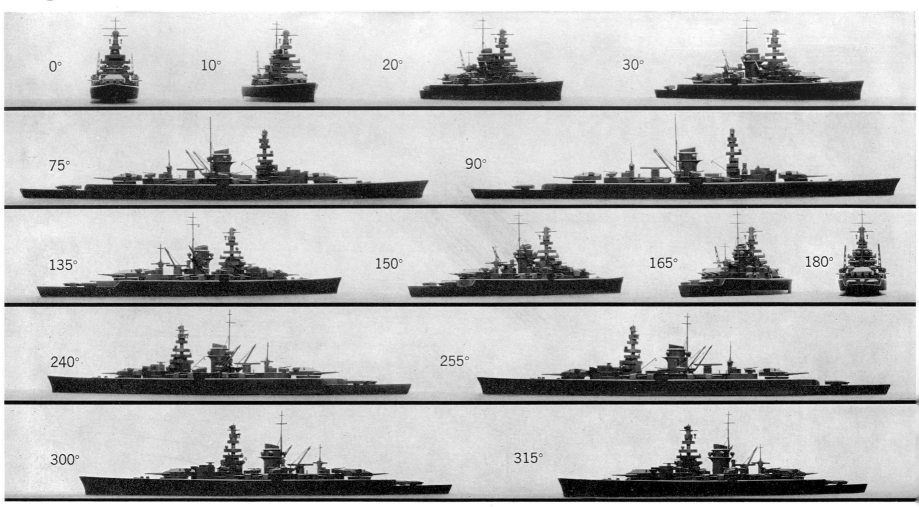

ONI 204

ADMIRAL SCHEER—CA 7

DIVISION OF NAVAL INTELLIGENCE—IDENTIFICATION AND CHARACTERISTICS SECTION—SEPTEMBER, 1942

BEGUN— SEPTEMBER 6, 1931
COMPLETED—NOVEMBER 12, 1934
SISTER SHIPS—LÜTZOW—CA6   ADMIRAL GRAF SPEE—CA8
(EX-DEUTSCHLAND)   (SUNK, DECEMBER 17, 1939)

ONI 204

RESTRICTED

1941

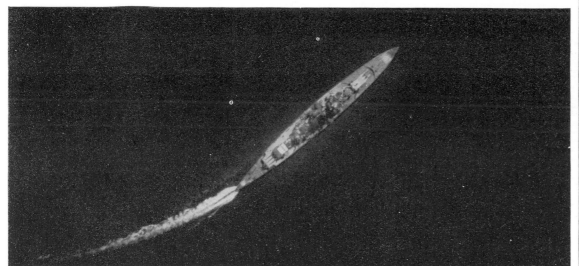

R.A.F.—APRIL 30, 1942

1941

HEIGHT OF OBSERVER

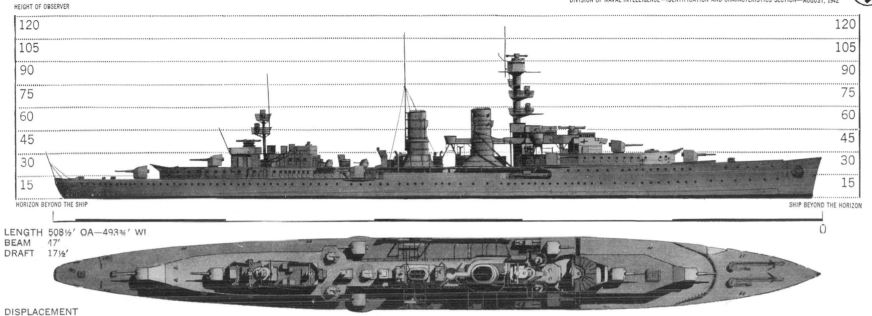

120	120
105	105
90	90
75	75
60	60
45	45
30	30
15	15

HORIZON BEYOND THE SHIP

SHIP BEYOND THE HORIZON

LENGTH 508½' OA—493¾' WI
BEAM 47'
DRAFT 17½'

0

DISPLACEMENT
5,400 TONS

DENSITY OF FIRE
MAIN BATTERY

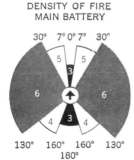

30°	7° 0° 7°	30°
	5	5
	3	
6	↑	6
	3	
	4	4
130°	160° 160°	130°
	180°	

ARMAMENT

	MAX. ELEV.	RANGE
8-5".9 SINGLE SHIELDS	27°	18,750 YD.
3-3".5 A.A.		
4-M.G.		
4-19".7 TORPEDO TUBES		

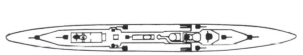

PROTECTION

BELT—2" AMIDSHIPS, TAPERING TO 1½" AT ENDS
TURRETS—NONE, WEATHER SHIELDS ONLY
CONNING TOWER—4"
SECONDARY BATTERY—3" TO 4" VERT. SIDES
2" GUN HOUSES

DECKS—1"

KNOTS	R.P.M
	420
	400
	350
	300
	275
	250
	245
	240
	220
	200
	160
	150
	120
	80

DES. SPD	DES. HP
29 KTS	46,500

EMDEN—CL1

DIVISION OF NAVAL INTELLIGENCE—IDENTIFICATION AND CHARACTERISTICS SECTION—AUGUST, 1942

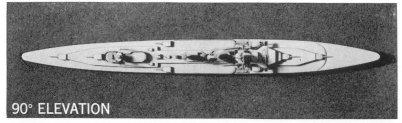

90° ELEVATION

PROFILE–2 STACKS
POLE FOREMAST
BROKEN HULL LINE

AERIAL–FLAT SIDED HULL
SINGLE MOUNT GUN SHIELDS

END-ON–
NARROW BRIDGE
TALL POLE FOREMAST

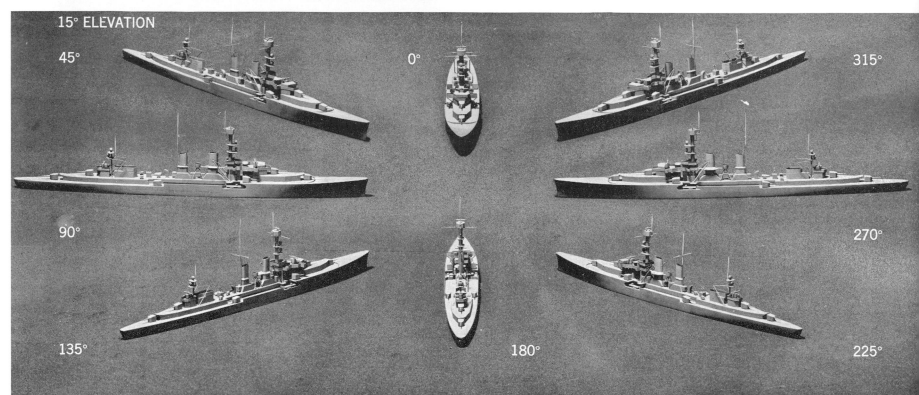

15° ELEVATION

45°   0°   315°

90°   270°

135°   180°   225°

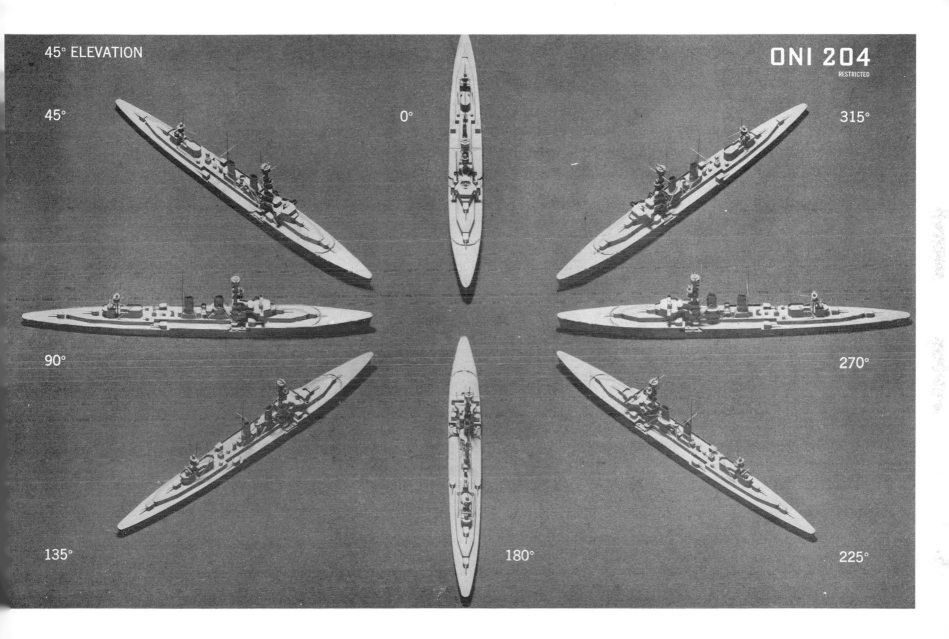

45° ELEVATION

ONI 204
RESTRICTED

45°   0°   315°

90°   270°

135°   180°   225°

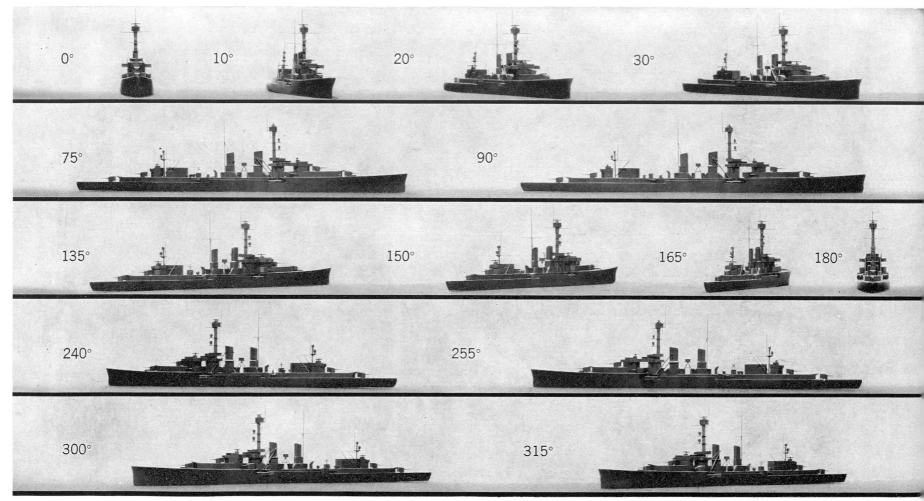

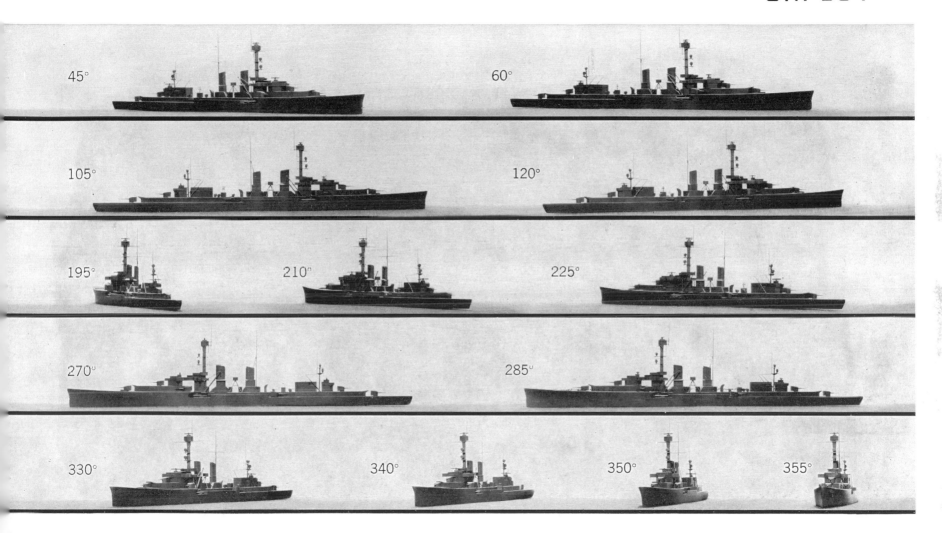

45°

60°

105°

120°

195°

210°

225°

270°

285°

330°

340°

350°

355°

EMDEN—CL1

DIVISION OF NAVAL INTELLIGENCE—IDENTIFICATION AND CHARACTERISTICS SECTION·—AUGUST. 1942

BEGUN—DECEMBER, 1921. COMPLETED—OCTOBER, 1925
USED AS SEA-GOING TRAINING SHIP FOR CADETS

ONI 204

RESTRICTED

FEBRUARY 8, 1936

R.A.F. 1941

FEBRUARY 8, 1936

DIVISION OF NAVAL INTELLIGENCE—IDENTIFICATION AND CHARACTERISTICS SECTION—AUGUST, 1942

HEIGHT OF OBSERVER

105	105
90	90
75	75
60	60
45	45
30	30
15	15

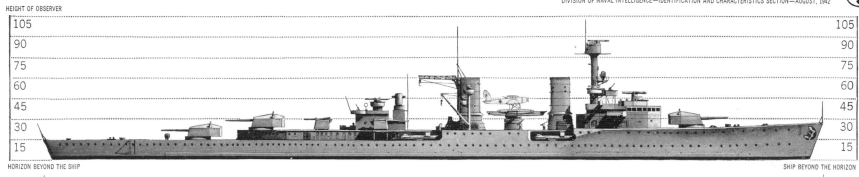

HORIZON BEYOND THE SHIP

SHIP BEYOND THE HORIZON

0

LENGTH 570'-10" OA—554'-5" WL
BEAM 49'-10"
DRAFT 17'-8" (FULL LOAD)

DISPLACEMENT
6,000 TONS (STANDARD)

DENSITY OF FIRE
MAIN BATTERY

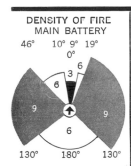

46°	10° 9° 19°	
	0°	

130° 180° 130°

ARMAMENT

		MAX. ELEV.	RANGE
9-5"9	TRIPLE TURRETS	40°	27,000 YD.
6-3"5	TWIN A.A. SHIELDS	80°	
18 (PLUS)	SMALLER A.A.		
12-21"	TORPEDO TUBES (TRIPLES)		
1 CATAPULT, 2 SEAPLANE SCOUTS			

PROTECTION

BELT—2" TAPERING TO 1½" AT ENDS
TURRETS—1½" FACE PLATES, 1¼" SIDES, ¾" BACK WALL
BARBETTES—
CONNING TOWER—3"—4"
DECKS—2" (MAX.)
POOR UNDERWATER PROTECTION

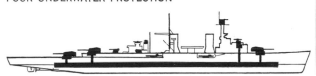

KNOTS	R.P.M.
	420
	400
	350
	300
	275
	260
	245
	240
	220
	200
	160
	150
	120
	80

DES. SPD   DES. HP
32 KTS   65,000

KÖLN—CL4

DIVISION OF NAVAL INTELLIGENCE—IDENTIFICATION AND CHARACTERISTICS SECTION—AUGUST, 1942

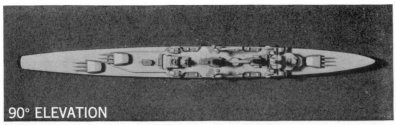

90° ELEVATION

PROFILE–2 STACKS
TRIPLE TURRETS—
1 FORWARD, 2 AFT

AERIAL–AFT TURRETS
STAGGERED

END-ON–
POLE FOREMAST
FULL-WIDTH BRIDGE WINGS

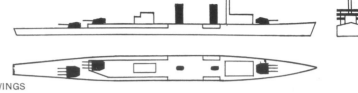

15° ELEVATION

45°   0°   315°

90°   270°

135°   180°   225°

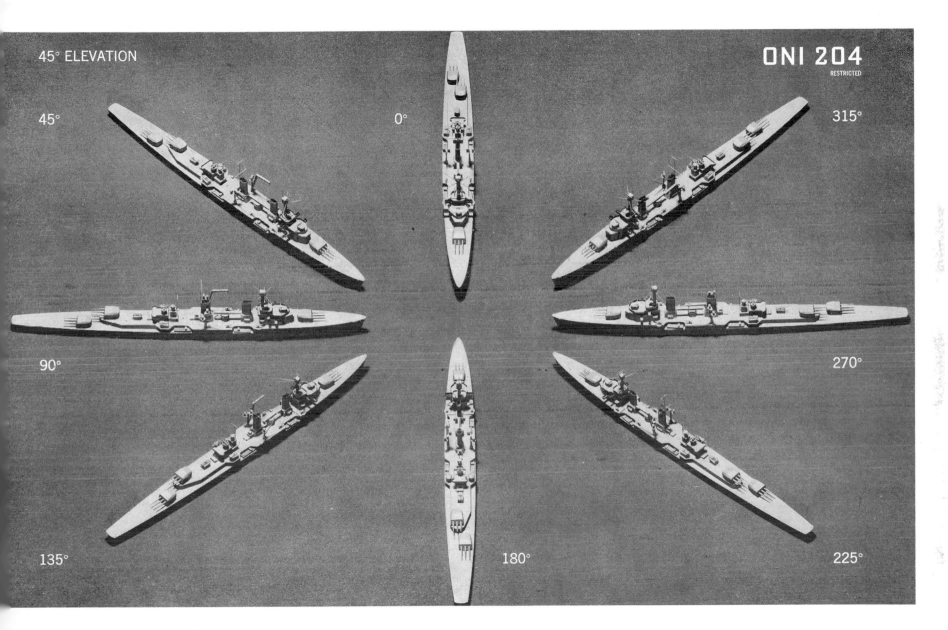

45° ELEVATION

ONI 204

RESTRICTED

45°

0°

315°

90°

270°

135°

180°

225°

KÖLN—CL4

DIVISION OF NAVAL INTELLIGENCE—IDENTIFICATION AND CHARACTERISTICS SECTION —AUGUST, 1942

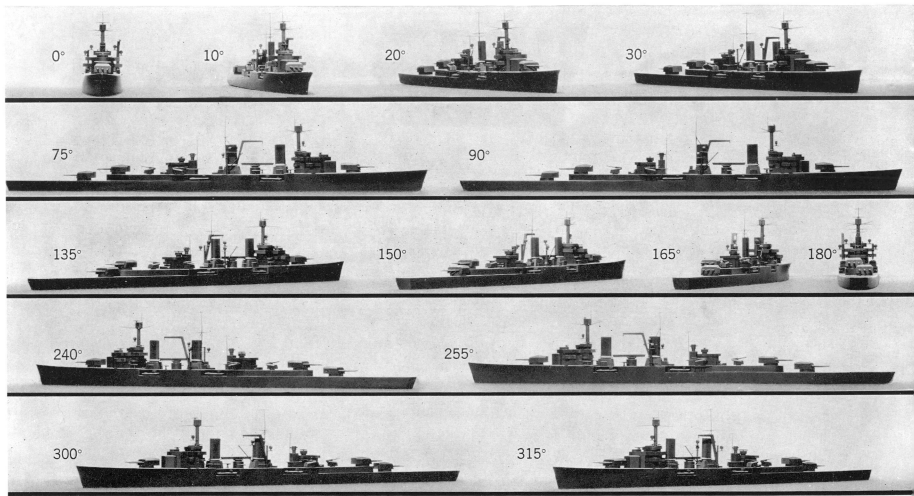

KÖLN—CL4
DIVISION OF NAVAL INTELLIGENCE—IDENTIFICATION AND CHARACTERISTICS SECTION—AUGUST, 1942

BEGUN—AUGUST 7, 1926.   COMPLETED—JANUARY 15, 1930
SISTER SHIPS—KARLSRUHE (SUNK), KOENIGSBERG (SUNK)

ONI 204
RESTRICTED

R.A.F. APRIL 20, 1939

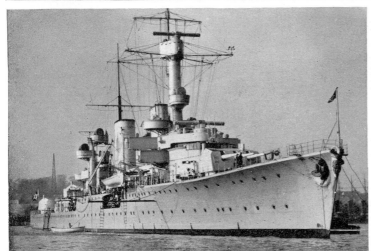

1934

HEIGHT OF OBSERVER

105	105
90	90
75	75
60	60
45	45
30	30
15	15

HORIZON BEYOND THE SHIP

SHIP BEYOND THE HORIZON

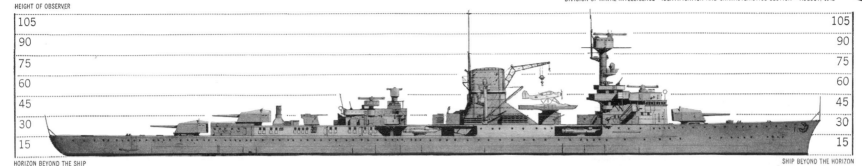

0

LENGTH 581' OA—554'-7" WL
BEAM 53'-5"
DRAFT 15'-7" (STANDARD)

DISPLACEMENT
6,000 TONS

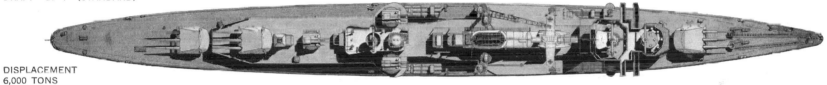

DENSITY OF FIRE MAIN BATTERY

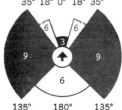

35° 18° 0° 18° 35°

6 6
3
9 9
6

135° 180° 135°

ARMAMENT

	MAX. ELEV.	RANGE
9-5"9 TRIPLE TURRETS	50°	20,000 YD.
6-3"5 H.A. TWIN TURRETS	80°	
8-1"46 A.A. TWIN TURRETS		
12-21" TORPEDO TUBES (TRIPLE)		
1 CATAPULT, 2 SEAPLANE SCOUTS		

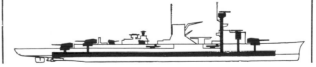

PROTECTION

BELT—4" BEHIND BULGE
TURRETS—1½" FACE PLATES—1¼" SIDES—¾" BACK WALL
BARBETTES—
F.C. TOWER—4"
SECONDARY BATTERY—
DECKS—¾" TO 1½"

KNOTS	RPM
32	400
29	350
26	300
22	250
20	245
18	200
13½	150

DES. SPD	DES. HP
32 KTS	TURBINES
	60,000
	DIESEL
	12,000

LEIPZIG—CL5

DIVISION OF NAVAL INTELLIGENCE—IDENTIFICATION AND CHARACTERISTICS SECTION·—AUGUST, 1942

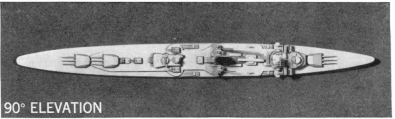

90° ELEVATION

PROFILE–TRUNK STACK
TURRETS—1 FRD.—2 AFT
CATAPULT FRD. OF STACK
AMIDSHIPS CRANE

PLAN–TRIPLE TURRETS
MINOR SUPERSTRUCTURE
AFT

END-ON—
FULL WIDTH BRIDGE
POLE FOREMAST

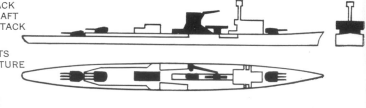

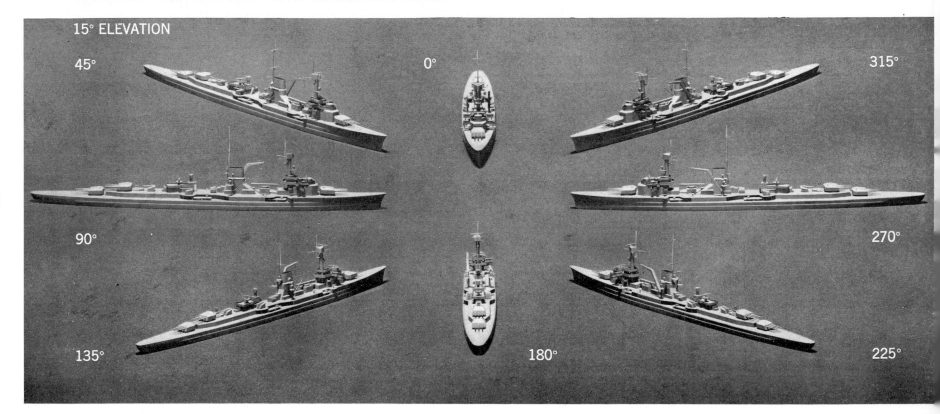

15° ELEVATION

45° 0° 315°

90° 270°

135° 180° 225°

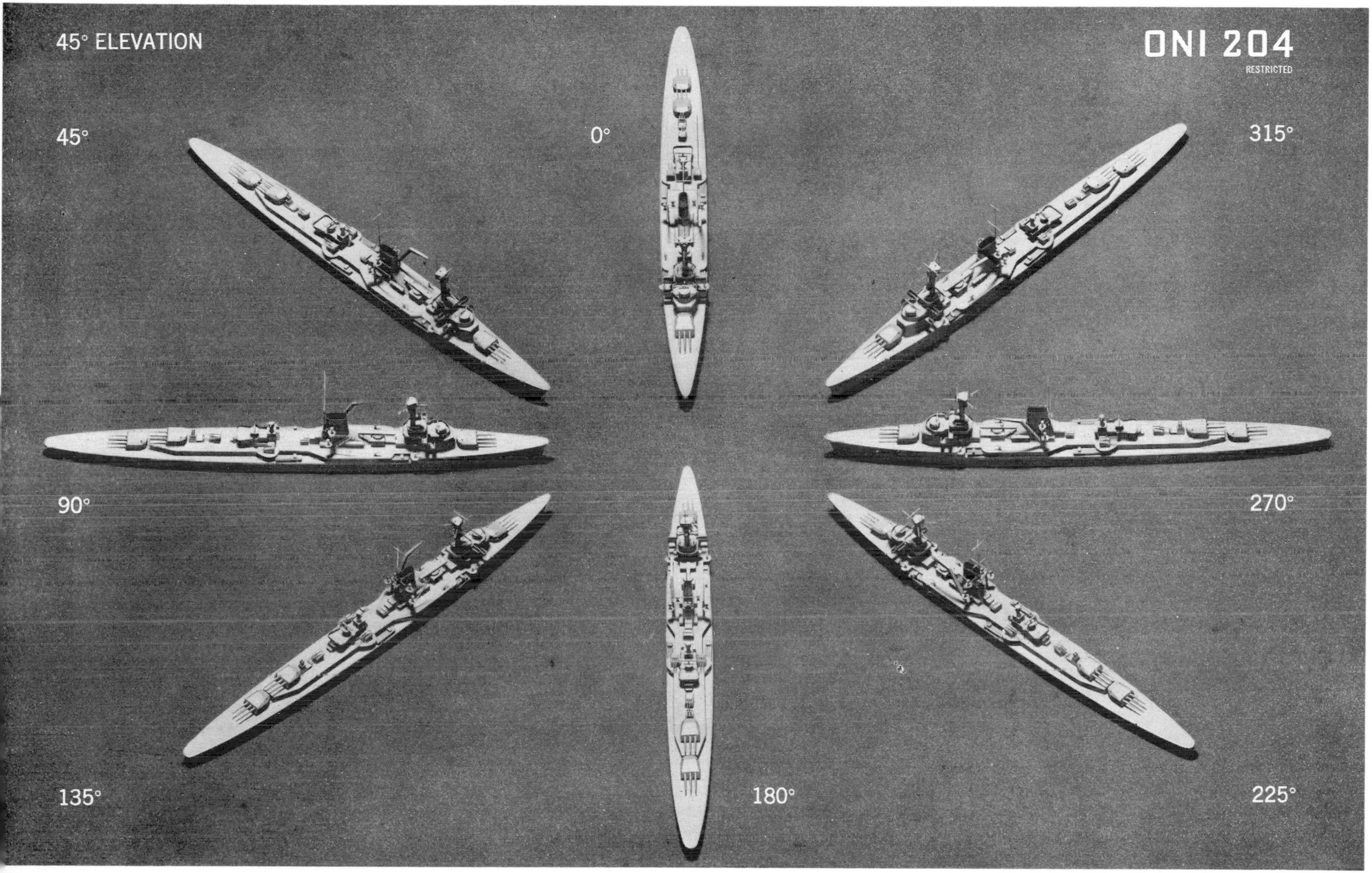

45°

0°

315°

90°

270°

135°

180°

225°

LEIPZIG—CL5

DIVISION OF NAVAL INTELLIGENCE—IDENTIFICATION AND CHARACTERISTICS SECTION—AUGUST, 1942

0° 10° 20° 30°

75° 90°

135° 150° 165° 180°

240° 255°

300° 315°

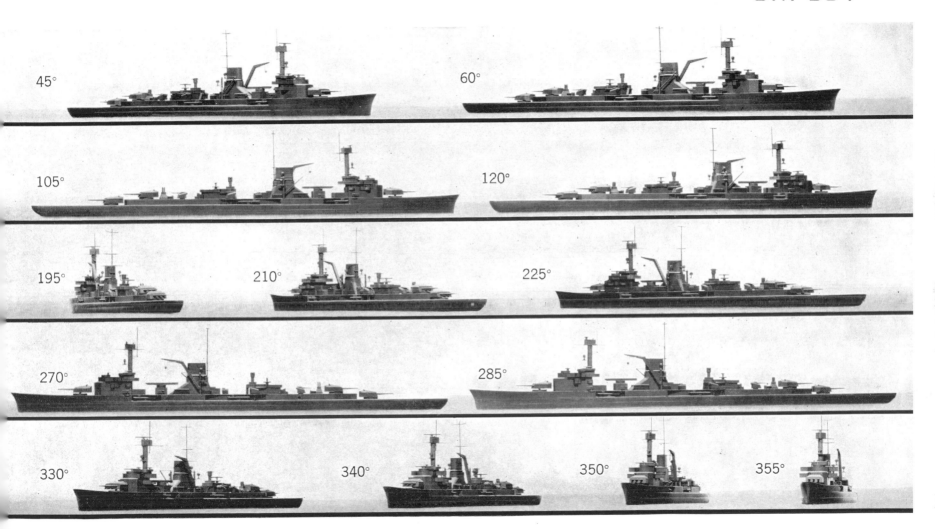

45°

60°

105°

120°

195°

210°

225°

270°

285°

330°

340°

350°

355°

OCTOBER, 1939

HEIGHT OF OBSERVER

105	105
90	90
75	75
60	60
45	45
30	30
15	15

HORIZON BEYOND THE SHIP

SHIP BEYOND THE HORIZON

0

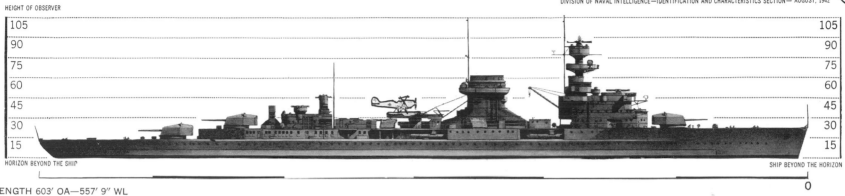

LENGTH 603′ OA—557′ 9″ WL
BEAM 54′
DRAFT 14′-3″ (MEAN)

DISPLACEMENT
6,000 TONS (STANDARD)

DENSITY OF FIRE
MAIN BATTERY

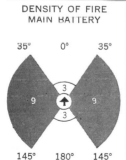

35°	0°	35°
	3	
9	↑	9
	3	
145°	180°	145°

ARMAMENT

	MAX. ELEV.	RANGE
9–5″9 TRIPLE TURRETS	50°	20,000 YD.
8–3″5 H.A. TWIN TURRETS	80°	
8–1″46 A.A. TWIN TURRETS		
12–21″ TORPEDO TUBES (TRIPLE)		
1 CATAPULT, 2 SCOUT OBSERVATION		

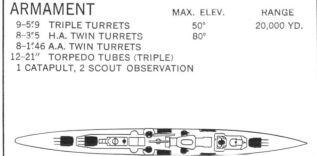

PROTECTION

BELT—1¾″ AMIDSHIP
TURRETS— 1½″ FACE PLATES
1¼″ SIDE PLATES
¾″ REAR WALL
BARBETTES—
F.C. TOWER—4″
DECKS— ¾″ TO 1½″
UNDER WATER PROTECTION VERY COMPLETE

KNOTS	R.P.M.
	420
	400
	350
	300
	275
	250
	225
	200
	175
	150
	125
	100

DES. SPD	DES. HP
32 KTS	72,000

NÜRNBERG—CL 6

DIVISION OF NAVAL INTELLIGENCE—IDENTIFICATION AND CHARACTERISTICS SECTION—AUGUST, 1942

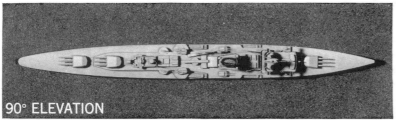

90° ELEVATION

PROFILE—TRUNK STACK
TURRETS—1 FRD.—2 AFT
CATAPULT ABAFT STACK

AERIAL—TRIPLE TURRETS
STACK SEARCHLIGHT
PLATFORM

END-ON
HIGH BRIDGE
NARROW BEAM

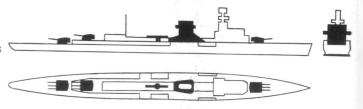

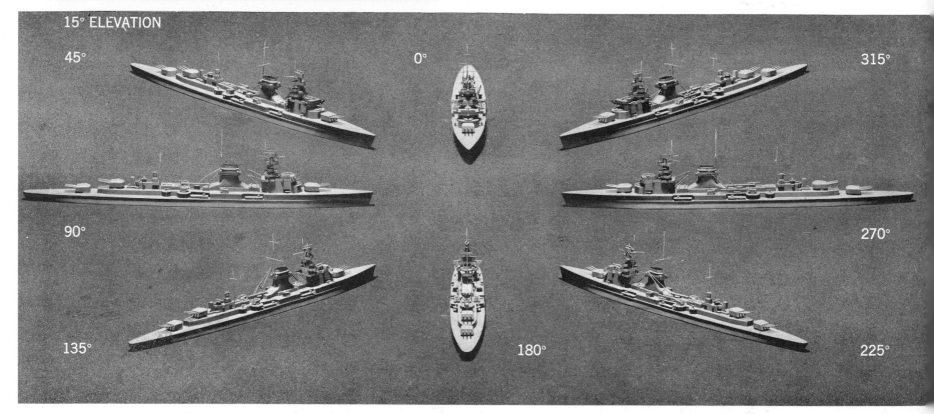

15° ELEVATION

45°   0°   315°

90°   270°

135°   180°   225°

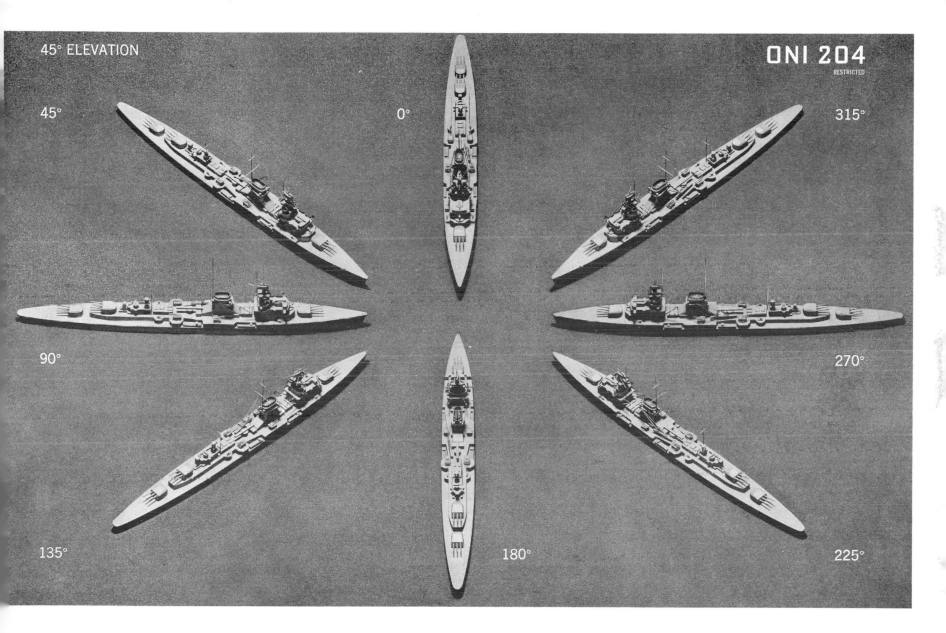

45°

0°

315°

90°

270°

135°

180°

225°

NÜRNBERG—CL6

DIVISION OF NAVAL INTELLIGENCE—IDENTIFICATION AND CHARACTERISTICS SECTION —AUGUST, 1942

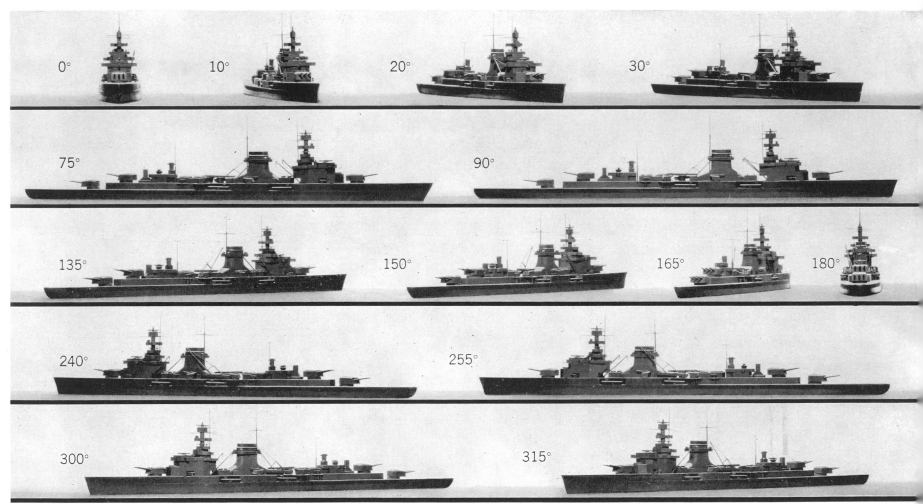

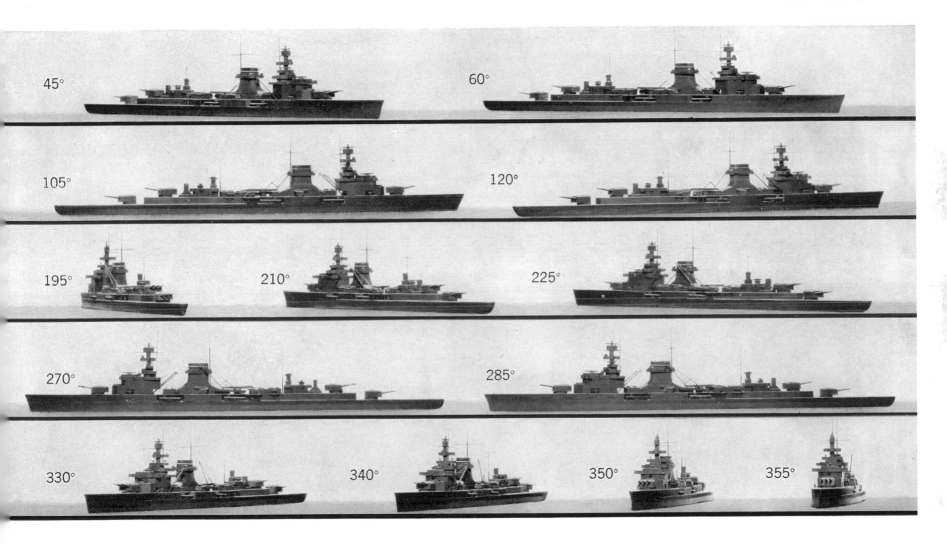

HEIGHT OF OBSERVER

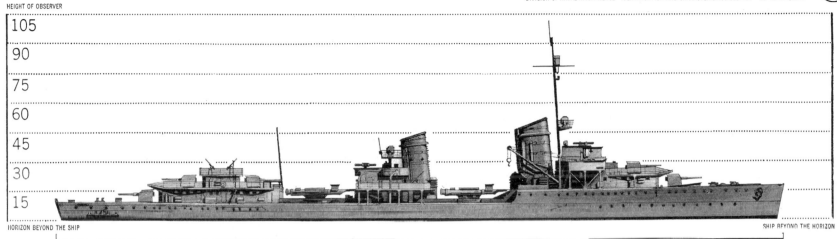

| 105 |
| 90 |
| 75 |
| 60 |
| 45 |
| 30 |
| 15 |

HORIZON BEYOND THE SHIP

SHIP BEYOND THE HORIZON

LENGTH—381' OA—374' WL
BEAM —37'-1"
DRAFT —9'-2" (MEAN)

0

DISPLACEMENT 1,625 TONS (STANDARD)

ARMAMENT

5–5"   GUN SHIELDS
4–1".46 AA
2–0".78 AA
8–21" TORPEDO TUBES (QUADRUPLE)
MAY CARRY MINES

PROPULSION

BOILERS–   H.P. WATER TUBE
DESIGNED H.P.–   50,000
DESIGNED SPEED–36 KTS.

KNOTS	R.P.M.
35	420
	400
30½	350
26¾	300
	275
23	250
	245
	240
	220
19	200
	160
14	150
	120
	80

MAASZ CLASS—DD4-16

DIVISION OF NAVAL INTELLIGENCE—IDENTIFICATION AND CHARACTERISTICS SECTION—SEPTEMBER, 1942

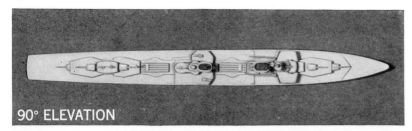

90° ELEVATION

MISTAKEN IDENTITY

MAASZ–DD 4-16　　　　WOLF–TB 7

15° ELEVATION

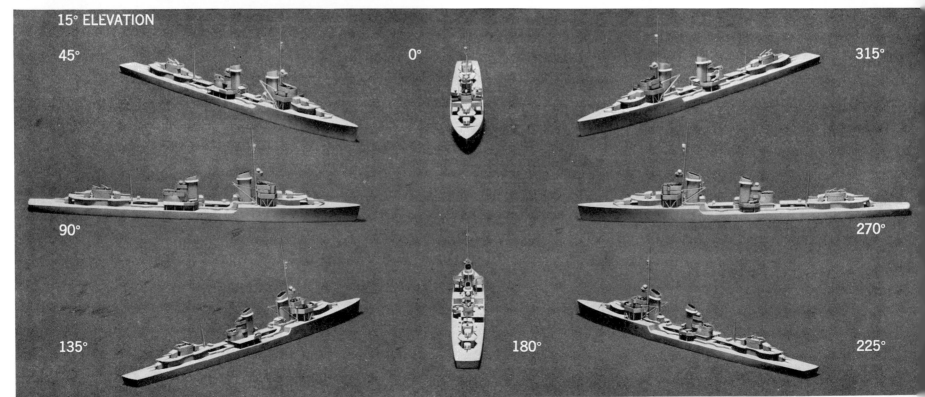

45°　　　0°　　　315°

90°　　　270°

135°　　　180°　　　225°

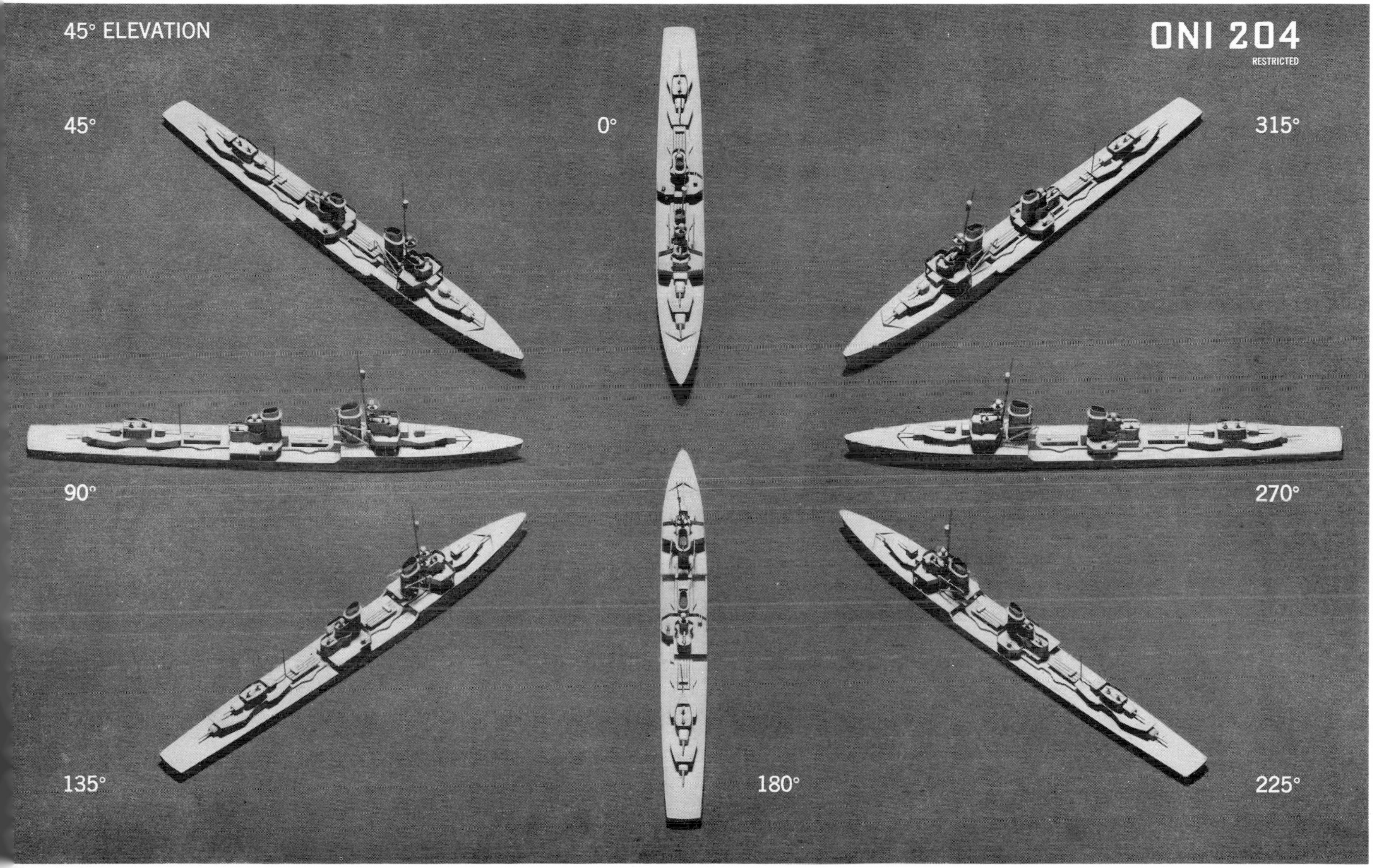

45°

0°

315°

90°

270°

135°

180°

225°

MAASZ CLASS—DD4-16

DIVISION OF NAVAL INTELLIGENCE—IDENTIFICATION AND CHARACTERISTICS SECTION—SEPTEMBER, 1942

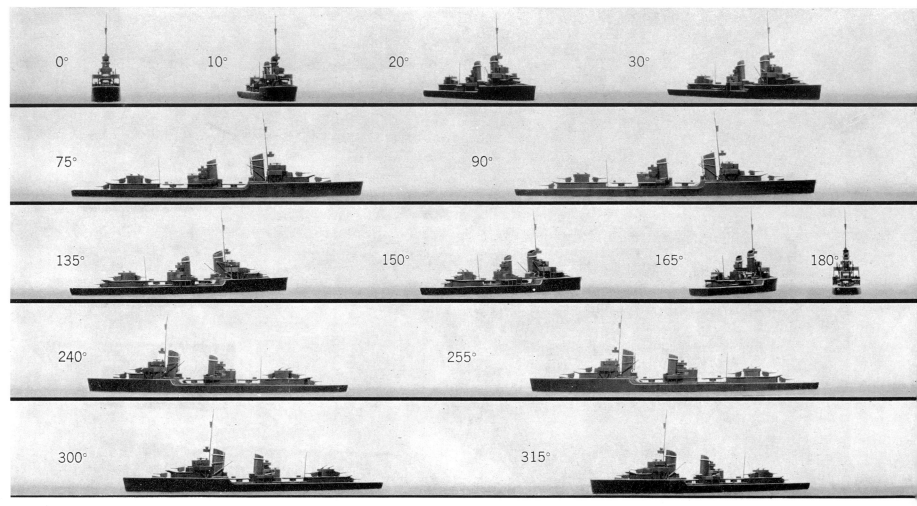

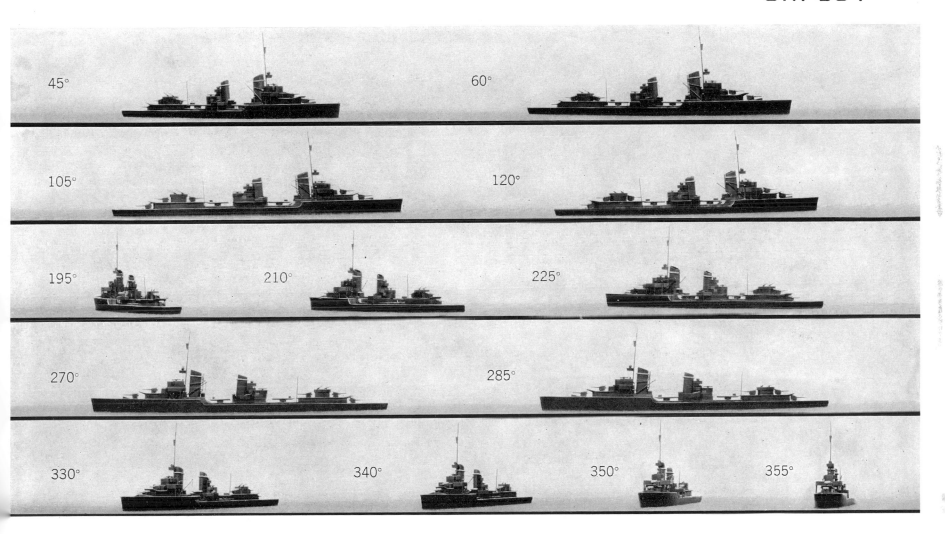

45°

60°

105°

120°

195°

210°

225°

270°

285°

330°

340°

350°

355°

SISTER SHIPS		BEGUN	COMPLETED				
RICHARD BEITZEN	−DD4	1935	5/13/37	HANS LODY	−DD10	1935	9/17/38
PAUL JACOBI	−DD5	7/15/35	6/29/37	FRIEDRICH IHN	−DD14	4/35	4/ 9/38
THEODOR RIEDEL	−DD6	7/18/35	7/ 6/37	ERICH STEINBRINCK	−DD15	4/35	6/ 8/38
HERMANN SCHOEMANN	−DD7	1935	9/15/37	FRIEDRICH ECKOLDT	−DD16	1935	8/ 2/38

PAUL JACOBI—1939 ▲

LEBERECHT MAASZ ▼

8/22/38 ▼

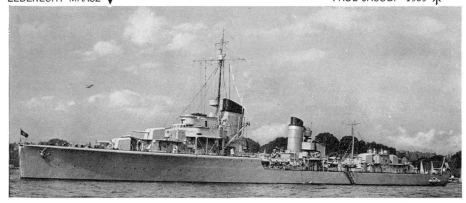

ARMAMENT

MAX. ELEV.   RANGE

5–5″   GUN SHIELDS
4–1″46 AA
2–0″78 AA
8–21″ TORPEDO TUBES (QUADRUPLE)
BELIEVED CAPABLE OF CARRYING MINES

PROPULSION

BOILERS	—HP WATER TUBE
MACHINERY	—GEARED TURBINE
FUEL	—OIL
DESIGNED SPEED	—36 KTS—35.5 KTS FULL SPEED (DEEP DRAFT)
DESIGNED HP	—55,000

KNOTS	R.P.M.	KNOTS	R.P.M.
	120		240
	400		220
	350		200
	300		160
	275		160
	250		120
	245		80

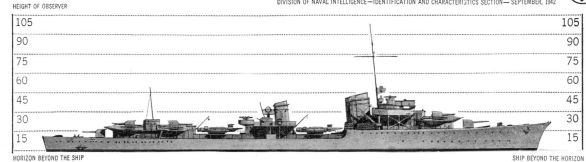

HEIGHT OF OBSERVER

HORIZON BEYOND THE SHIP

SHIP BEYOND THE HORIZON

LENGTH—399′ 6″ OA—385′ 6″ WL
BEAM —38′ 5″
DRAFT —9′ 6″ (STANDARD)

0

DISPLACEMENT—1,811 TONS
(STANDARD)

DEVELOPMENT OF THE MAASZ DESIGN;
REPORTED REFITTED AS IMPROVED ROEDER CLASS

1939

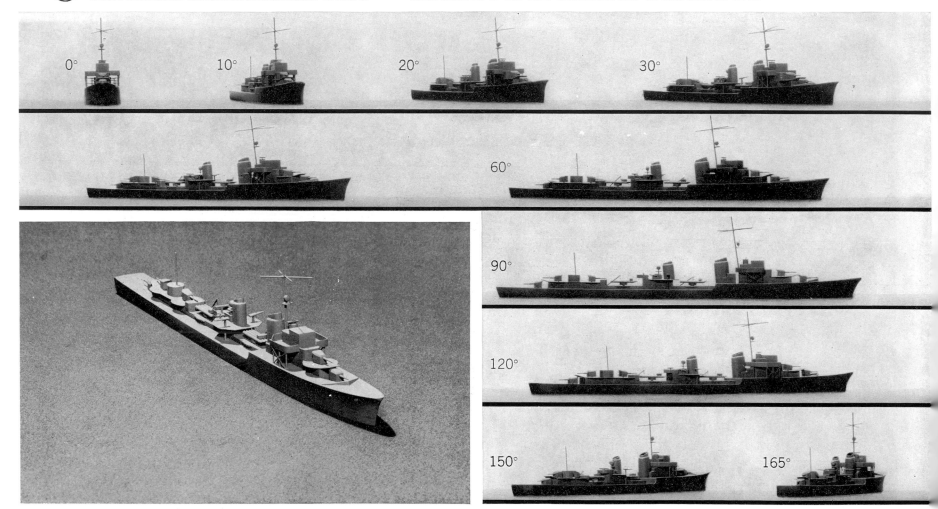

HEIGHT OF OBSERVER

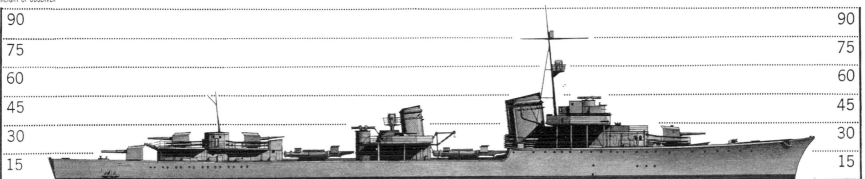

HORIZON BEYOND THE SHIP

SHIP BEYOND THE HORIZON

LENGTH 410' OA—385'-6" WL
BEAM 39'-4"
DRAFT 9'-6" (MEAN)

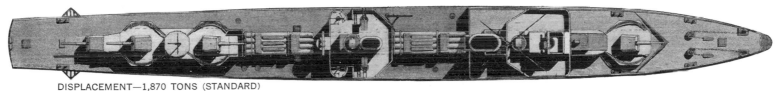

DISPLACEMENT—1,870 TONS (STANDARD)

ARMAMENT

4–5."9 GUN SHIELDS
4–1."46 AA
4–0."78 MG
8–21" TORPEDO TUBES (QUADRUPLE)
    SOME BOATS HAVE 6 TUBES, TRIPLED

PROPULSION

DESIGNED H.P.—55,000
DESIGNED SPEED—36 KTS.

NOTES

SLIGHTLY ENLARGED ROEDERS; DISTINGUISH-ABLE BY A SINGLE SHIELD GUN FORWARD.

5."9 GUN BATTERY ADOPTED TO ENGAGE OPPOS-ING CRUISERS IN NORWEGIAN WATERS: GERMANS REPORTED REFERRING TO THEM AS "CONVOY DESTROYERS."

ADDITIONAL GERMAN DESTROYERS OF IDENTI-CAL DIMENSIONS HAVE BEEN OBSERVED; DESIGN CLASSES, NAMES AND NUMBERS UNREPORTED. SOME MOUNT A TWIN GUN HOUSE FORWARD WITH LIGHT AA IN LIEU OF A SHIELD GUN ON THE FANTAIL; OTHERS HAVE SUPERFIRING GUNS FORE AND AFT WITH LIGHT AA ABAFT 2ND NEST OF TUBES.

KTS.	R.P.M.
	420
	400
	350
	300
	275
	245
	240
	220
	200
	160
	150
	120
	80

"NARVIK" CLASS—DD 23-43

DIVISION OF NAVAL INTELLIGENCE—IDENTIFICATION AND CHARACTERISTICS SECTION·—AUGUST, 1942

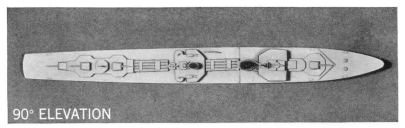

90° ELEVATION

MISTAKEN IDENTITY

KARL GALSTER   NARVIK CLASS

15° ELEVATION

45°   0°   315°

90°   270°

135°   180°   225°

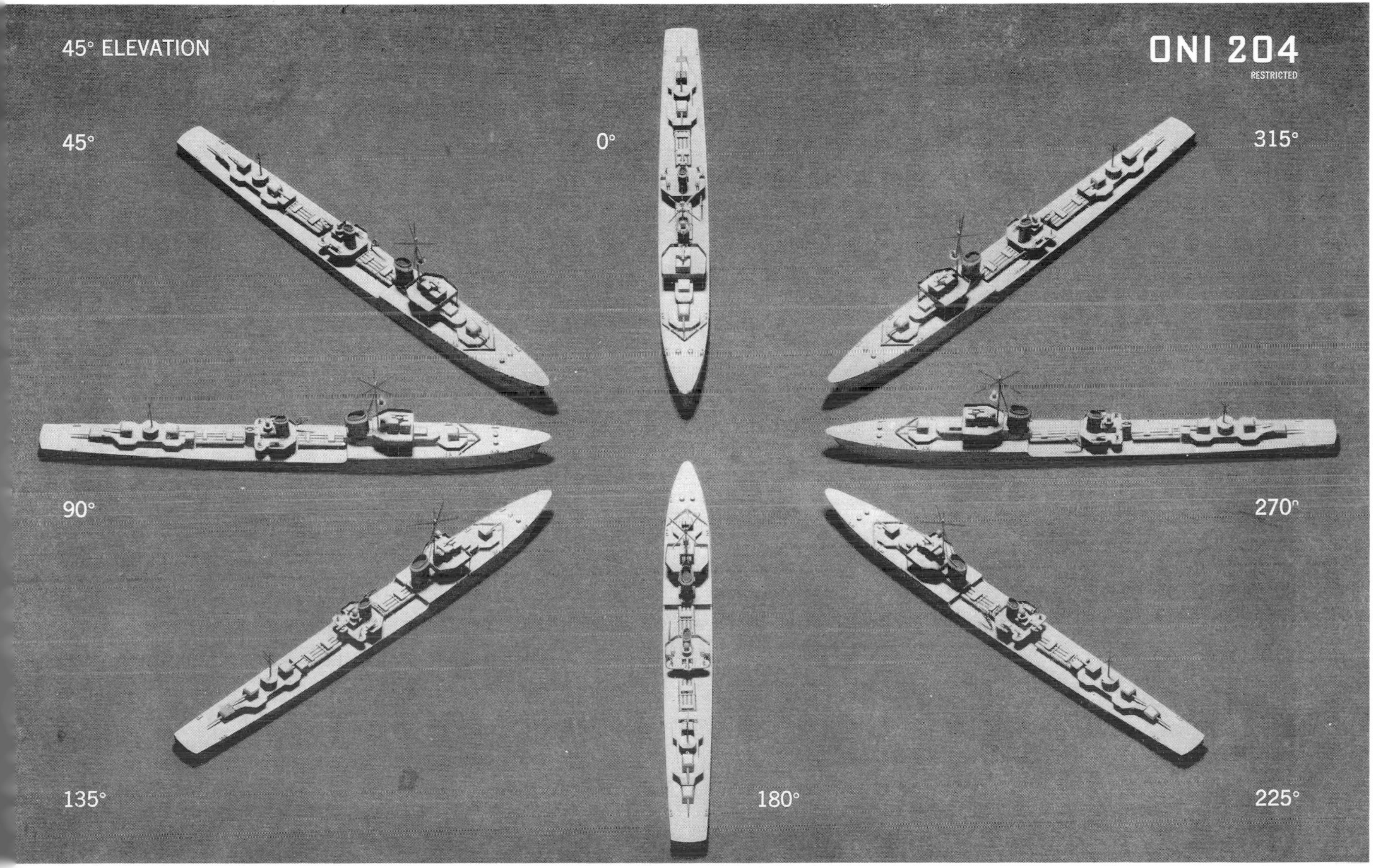

0°

45°

315°

90°

270°

135°

180°

225°

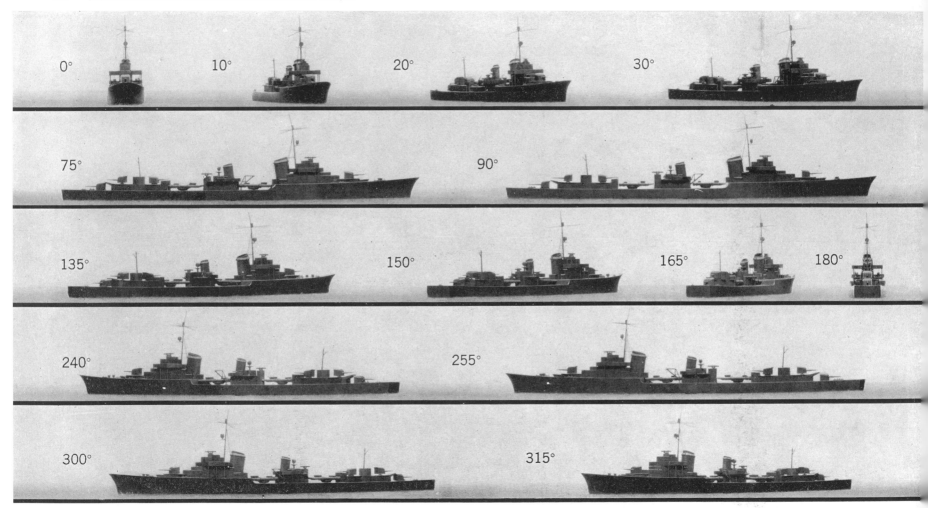

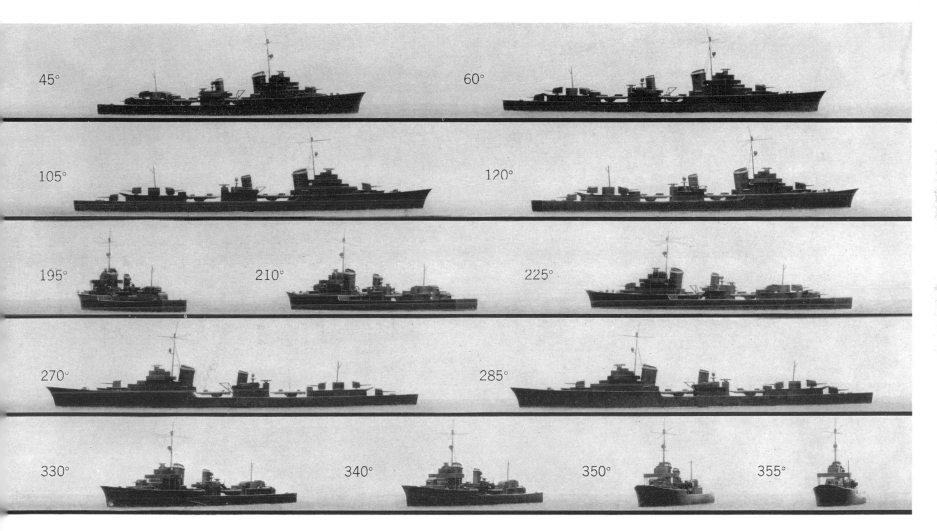

45°

60°

105°

120°

195°

210°

225°

270°

285°

330°

340°

350°

355°

"NARVIK" CLASS—DD 23-43

DIVISION OF NAVAL INTELLIGENCE—IDENTIFICATION AND CHARACTERISTICS SECTION—AUGUST, 1942

BEGUN–1939.   COMPLETED–1940
NAMES AND NUMBERS UNREPORTED; "NARVIK" IS TEMPORARY CLASS DES-
IGNATION DERIVED FROM A "NARVIK FLOTILLA" COMPRISED OF THESE BOATS.
SISTER SHIPS–Z-23 (BRUNO HEINEMAN)   Z-24-43

ONI 204

RESTRICTED

PHOTOS–1941

TJERK HIDDES DD-48
GERARD CALLENBURG DD-47
EX-DUTCH

LAUNCHED — OCTOBER 12, 1939

SUNK— RAISED AND BEING COMPLETED BY GERMANS

DIMENSIONS—
LENGTH—348'-9"OA
BEAM — 33'-9"
DRAFT — 11'-6" (MAXIMUM)
10'-2" (MEAN)

DISPLACEMENT—
1,628 TONS (STANDARD)
1,922 TONS (NORMAL)

ARMAMENT— 5-4".7 (2 TWINS, 1 SINGLE);
4-1".57 (TWINS); 4 MG
TORPEDO TUBES—8-21"
24 MINES—
AIRCRAFT— 1 FP, 1

PROPULSION—
H.P. — 45,000 (DES.)
SPEED — 36 KNOTS (DES.)
ENDURANCE— 7,000 @ 15 KNOTS (EST)

NOS. 1 & 2 DD-45, 46
EX-NORWEGIAN

LAUNCHED — BELIEVED TO BE DURING 1941
CONSTRUCTION BEING EXPEDITED BY
GERMANS

DIMENSIONS—
LENGTH—319' OA
BEAM — 32'-10"
DRAFT — 9'-1" (MAXIMUM)

DISPLACEMENT—
1,200 TONS (STANDARD)

ARMAMENT— 4-4".7; 2-1".57 AA; 2-0".5 MG
TORPEDO TUBES—4-21"

PROPULSION—
H.P. —30,000 (DES.)
SPEED—36 KNOTS

BASILEUS GIORGIOS I DD-55
EX-GREEK

COMPLETED— DECEMBER 27, 1938

SUNK— BELIEVED RAISED BY GERMANS
AND FITTED FOR MINE SWEEPING

DIMENSIONS—
LENGTH—323'-1" OA-320' WL
BEAM — 33'
DRAFT — 14'-5" (MAXIMUM)
8'-9" (MEAN)

DISPLACEMENT—
1,420 TONS (STANDARD)

ARMAMENT— 4-5", 30°; 4-1".46 AA
8-0".52 AA
TORPEDO TUBES—8-21"

PROPULSION—
H.P. —34,000 (DES.)
SPEED —35.5 KNOTS (DES.)
ENDURANCE—4,670 @ 10 KNOTS
4,870 @ 15 KNOTS
1,040 @ MAX. CONT.
SEA-GOING SPEED
980 @ FULL SPEED

L'ALSACIEN DD-51

LE CORSE DD-52

EX-FRENCH

SEIZED— ON WAYS, BELIEVED BEING
COMPLETED

DIMENSIONS—
LENGTH—295'-3" WL
BEAM — 30'-5"
DRAFT — 8'-6" (MEAN)

DISPLACEMENT—
994 TONS (STANDARD)

ARMAMENT—4-3".9; 4-1".46 AA
TORPEDO TUBES—4-21".7

PROPULSION—
H.P. —28,000 (DES.)
SPEED—34 KNOTS (DES.)
L'ALSACIEN, LE CORSE

L'OPINIATRE DD-53

EX-FRENCH

SEIZED— ON WAYS, BELIEVED BEING
COMPLETED

DIMENSIONS—
LENGTH—363'-2" WL
BEAM — 36'-2"
DRAFT — 10'-2" (MEAN)

DISPLACEMENT—
1,772 TONS (STANDARD)

ARMAMENT—6-5".1, ME 36°, R. 18,600;
2-1".46 AA
TORPEDO TUBES—7-21".7 (1 TRIPLE &
2 DOUBLE MOUNTS)

PROPULSION—
H.P. —58,000 (DES.)
SPEED—35 KNOTS (DES.)

WICHER DD-44

EX-POLISH

COMPLETED—MARCH 21, 1931

SUNK— 1939, BELIEVED SALVAGED

DIMENSIONS—
LENGTH—339'-7"
BEAM — 33'-4"
DRAFT — 10'-2" (MAXIMUM)

DISPLACEMENT—
1,654 TONS (NORMAL)

ARMAMENT—4-5".1; 1-2".9 AA
TORPEDO TUBES—6-21".7
40 MINES
2 D. C. THROWERS

PROPULSION—
H.P. —33,000 (DES.)
SPEED —33 KNOTS (DES.)
ENDURANCE—3,000 @ 15 KNOTS

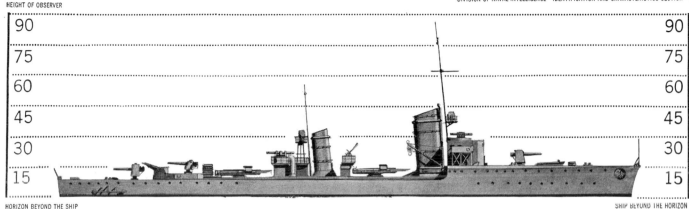

HEIGHT OF OBSERVER

90	90
75	75
60	60
45	45
30	30
15	15

HORIZON BEYOND THE SHIP

SHIP BEYOND THE HORIZON

LENGTH—287'-11" OA
277'-9" WL
BEAM— 27'-5"
DRAFT— 9'-2" (MAXIMUM)

DISPLACEMENT
800 TONS (STANDARD)

ARMAMENT
	MAX. ELEV.	RANGE
3-4."1 50 CAL.	80°	
2-1."18 AA		
2 MG		
6-21" TORPEDO TUBES (TRIPLE)		

PROPULSION
BOILERS—	3 SCHULTZ-THORNYCROFT "MARINE" TYPE
FUEL—	OIL
DESIGNED H.P.—	24,000
DESIGNED SPEED-	33 KTS.
ENDURANCE—	2,000 AT 20 KTS.

NOTES
BUILT AS "DESTROYER"; CONSIDERED UNSATISFACTORY FOR DESTROYER WORK AND A COSTLY FAILURE. COULD NOT STAND WINTER GALES.

COMPARTMENTATION AND DAMAGE CONTROL HIGHLY DEVELOPED, PRESUMABLY WITH A VIEW TO BALTIC OPERATION.

KNOTS	R.P.M.
	420
	400
	350
	300
	275
	250
	245
	240
	220
	200
	160
	150
	120
	80

MÖWE CLASS—TB1-6

DIVISION OF NAVAL INTELLIGENCE—IDENTIFICATION AND CHARACTERISTICS SECTION—SEPTEMBER, 1942

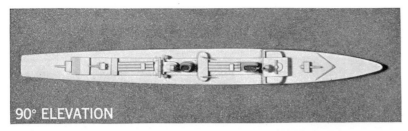

90° ELEVATION

MISTAKEN IDENTITY

MÖWE TB 1-6

WOLF TB 7

15° ELEVATION

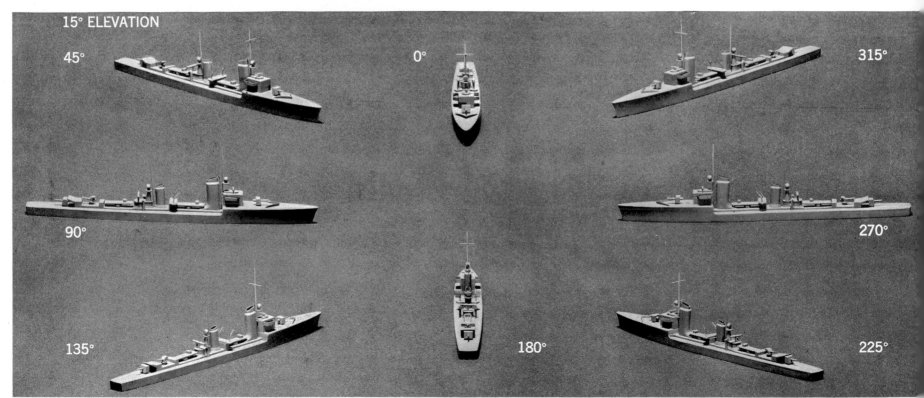

45°

0°

315°

90°

270°

135°

180°

225°

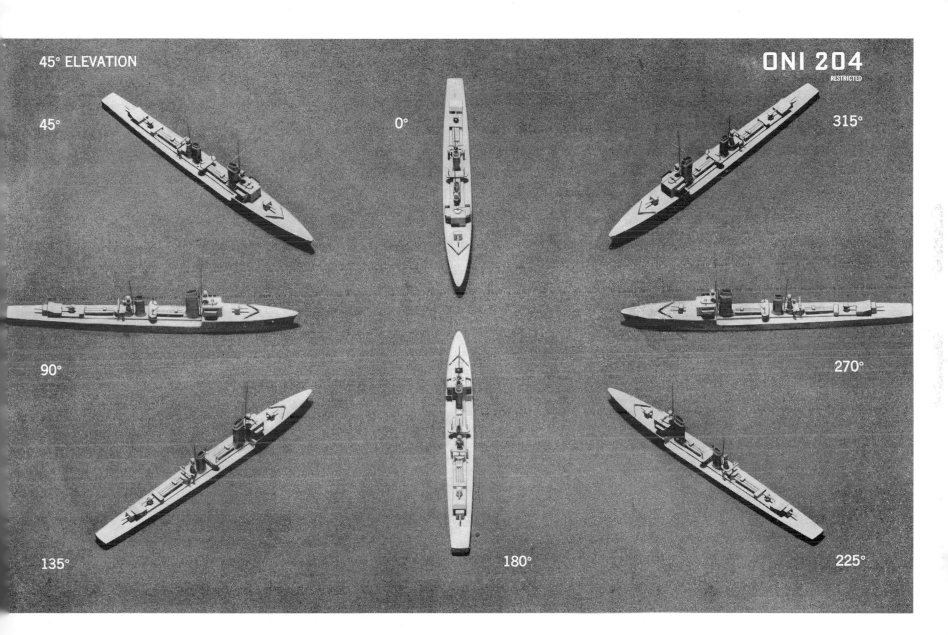

45° ELEVATION

ONI 204
RESTRICTED

45°

0°

315°

90°

270°

135°

180°

225°

MÖWE CLASS—TB1-6

DIVISION OF NAVAL INTELLIGENCE—IDENTIFICATION AND CHARACTERISTICS SECTION—SEPTEMBER, 1942

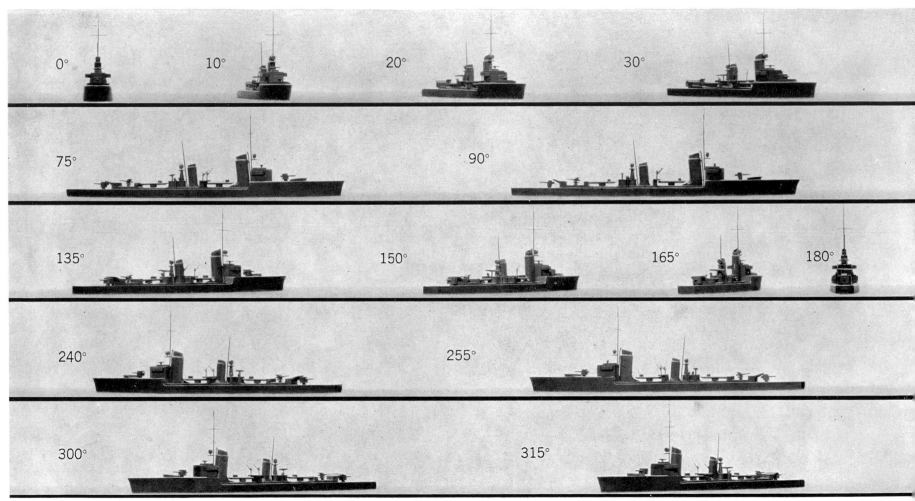

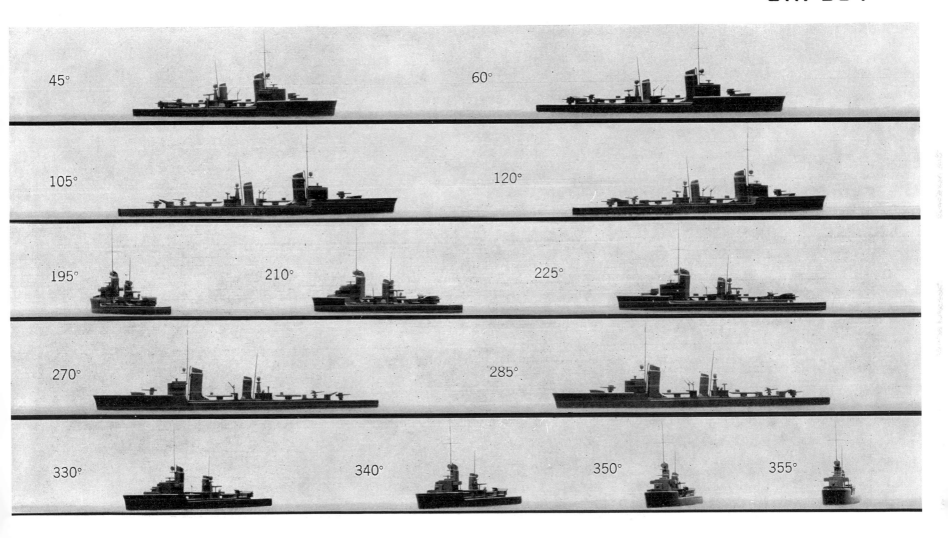

MÖWE CLASS—TB1-6

DIVISION OF NAVAL INTELLIGENCE—IDENTIFICATION AND CHARACTERISTICS SECTION—SEPTEMBER, 1942

SISTER SHIPS		BEGUN	COMPLETED					
MÖWE	TB 1	1925	10/1/26		FALKE	TB 5	12/7/25	8/1/27
GREIF	TB 3	10/5/25	3/17/27		KONDOR	TB 6	12/7/25	7/15/28
SEEADLER	TB 4	10/5/25	5/1/27					

ONI 204

RESTRICTED

HEIGHT OF OBSERVER

90	90
75	75
60	60
45	45
30	30
15	15

HORIZON BEYOND THE SHIP

SHIP BEYOND THE HORIZON

LENGTH 304' OA—292' WL
BEAM 28'-3"
DRAFT 8'-8" (MAXIMUM)

DISPLACEMENT
800 TONS (STANDARD)

ARMAMENT
MAX. ELEV. RANGE

3-4".1 DP SHIELDS 70°
2-1".18 AA
6 21" TORPEDO TUBES (TRIPLE)

PROPULSION

BOILERS-	3 SCHULTZ-THORNYCROFT "MARINE" TYPE
FUEL-	OIL 338 TONS
DESIGNED H.P.-	25,000
DESIGNED SPEED-	34 KNOTS
ENDURANCE-	2,200 AT 20 KTS

NOTES

BUILT AS A "DESTROYER" UNDER TERMS OF VERSAILLES TREATY. UNSATISFACTORY FOR DESTROYER WORK.

REPORTED TO HAVE BOW RUDDER.

KNOTS	R.P.M
	420
	400
	350
	300
	275
	250
	245
	240
	220
	200
	160
	150
	120
	80

WOLF CLASS—TB 7-12

DIVISION OF NAVAL INTELLIGENCE—IDENTIFICATION AND CHARACTERISTICS SECTION—SEPTEMBER, 1942

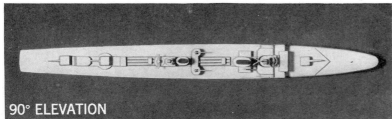

90° ELEVATION

MISTAKEN IDENTITY

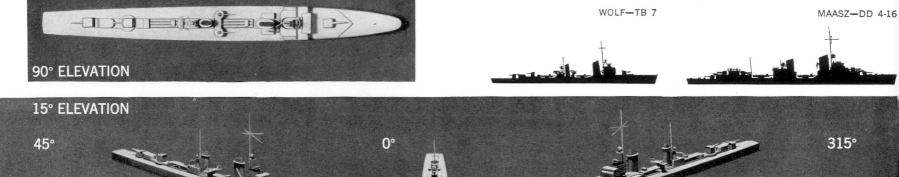

WOLF—TB 7

MAASZ—DD 4-16

15° ELEVATION

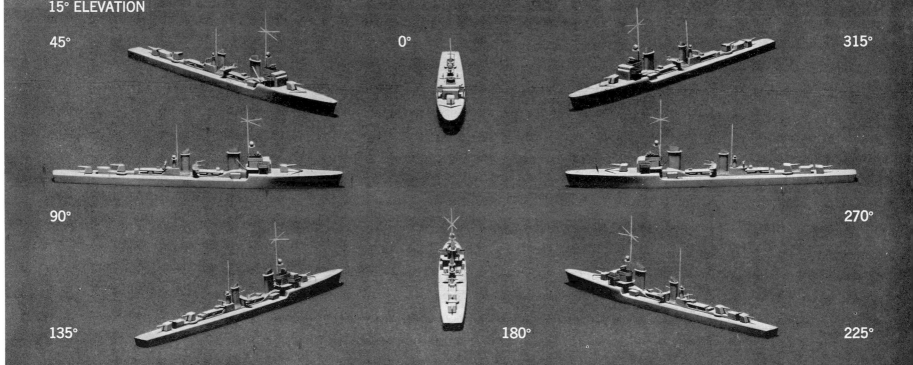

45°

0°

315°

90°

270°

135°

180°

225°

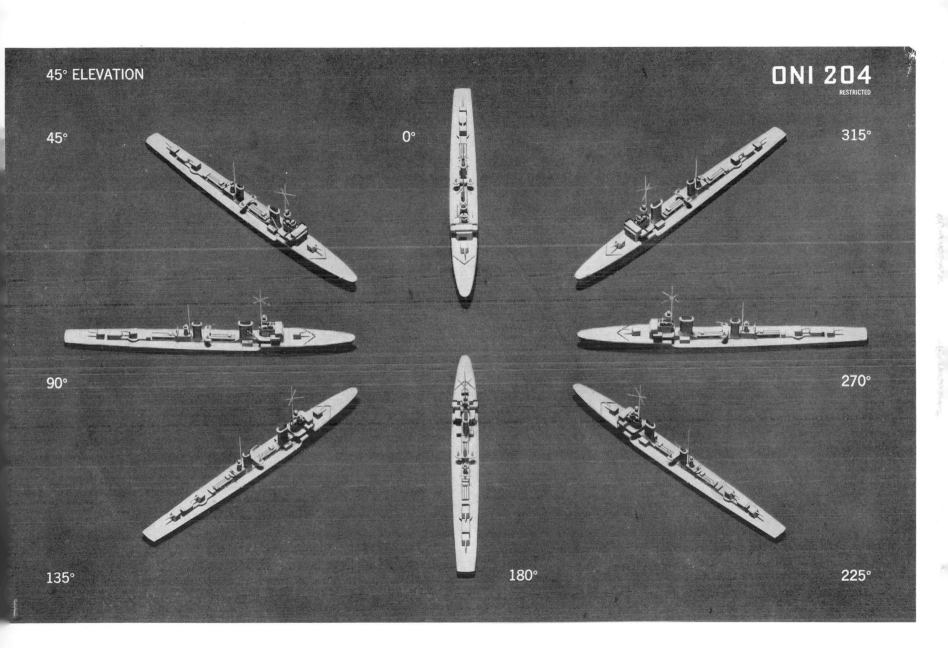

45° ELEVATION

ONI 204

RESTRICTED

45°

0°

315°

90°

270°

135°

180°

225°

WOLF CLASS—TB 7-12

DIVISION OF NAVAL INTELLIGENCE—IDENTIFICATION AND CHARACTERISTICS SECTION—SEPTEMBER, 1942

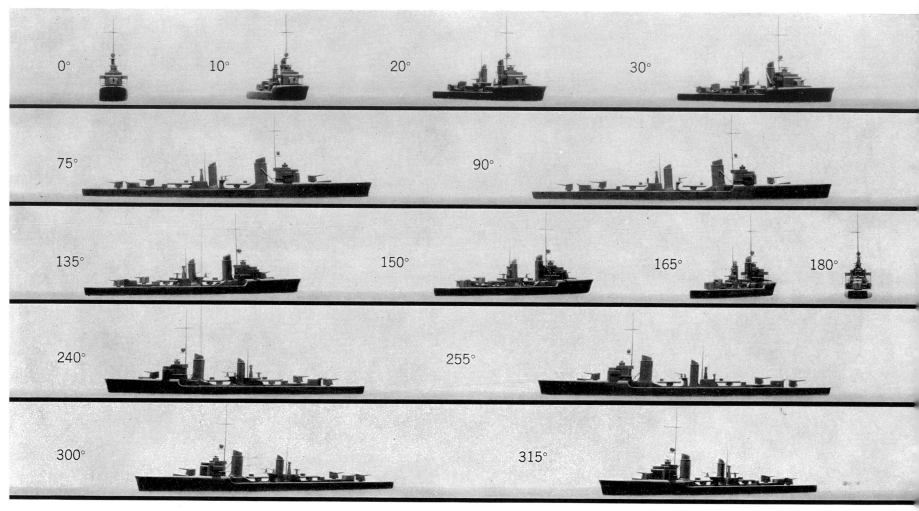

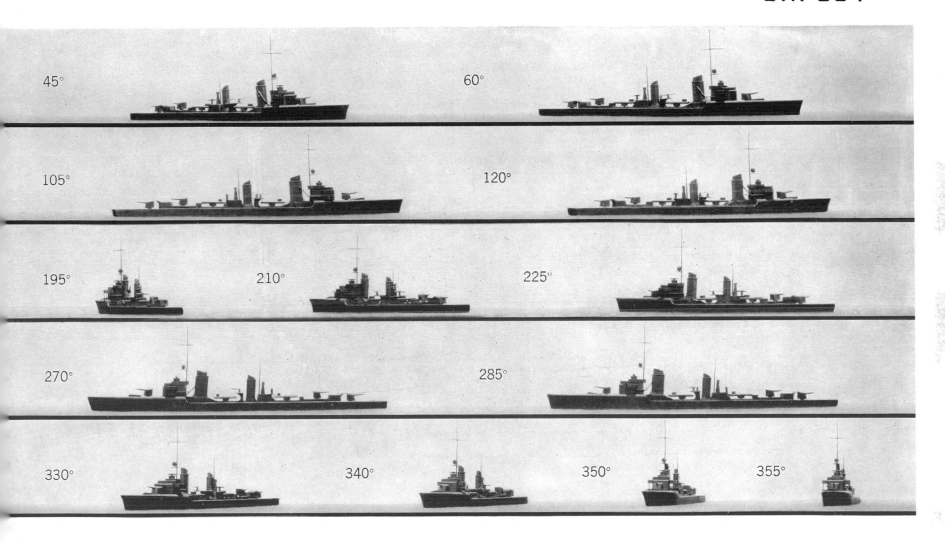

45°   60°

105°   120°

195°   210°   225°

270°   285°

330°   340°   350°   355°

WOLF CLASS—TB 7-12

DIVISION OF NAVAL INTELLIGENCE—IDENTIFICATION AND CHARACTERISTICS SECTION—SEPTEMBER, 1942

SISTER SHIPS		BEGUN	COMPLETED				
ILTIS	TB 8	3/19/27	10/1/28	LEOPARD	TB 10	5/ –/27	8/15/29
JAGUAR	TB 9	5/ –/27	6/1/29	TIGER	TB 12	3/26/27	1/15/29

ONI 204

RESTRICTED

WOLF, ILTIS & TIGER—JUNE 1937 ↓   TIGER—1931 ↑   LEOPARD 6/16/41 ↓

HEIGHT OF OBSERVER

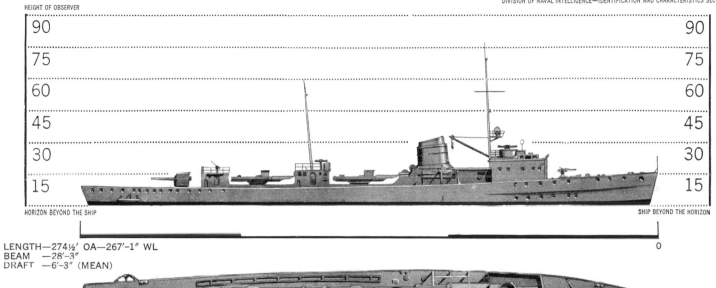

90	90
75	75
60	60
45	45
30	30
15	15

HORIZON BEYOND THE SHIP

SHIP BEYOND THE HORIZON

LENGTH—274½' OA—267'-1" WL
BEAM —28'-3"
DRAFT —6'-3" (MEAN)

0

DISPLACEMENT
600 TONS (STANDARD)

ARMAMENT

1-4".1
1-1".46
1 M.G.
6-21" TORPEDO TUBES

PROPULSION

GEARED TURBINES
HIGH PRESSURE WATER TUBE
 BOILERS
H.P.—22,000
DESIGNED SPEED—36 KNOTS

NOTES

EMPLOYMENT
—SCREENING MAJOR SURFACE UNITS
—"STIFFENING" COASTAL CONVOY
 ESCORTS AND PATROL FLOTILLAS
—COVER **AM** AND AIRCRAFT RESCUE
 VESSELS

DANGEROUS OPPONENTS AT LOW VISI-
BILITY BECAUSE OF LOW SILHOUETTE
AND HEAVY TORPEDO BATTERY

KTS.	R.P.M.
	480
	460
	440
	420
	400
	380
	360
	340
	320
	300
	280
	260
	240
	220
	200
	180
	160
	140

T1 CLASS—TB 13-31

DIVISION OF NAVAL INTELLIGENCE—IDENTIFICATION AND CHARACTERISTICS SECTION—AUGUST, 1942

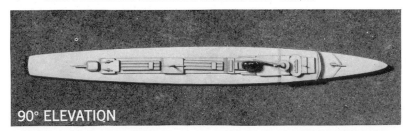

90° ELEVATION

MISTAKEN IDENTITY

T-1 CLASS

M-1 CLASS

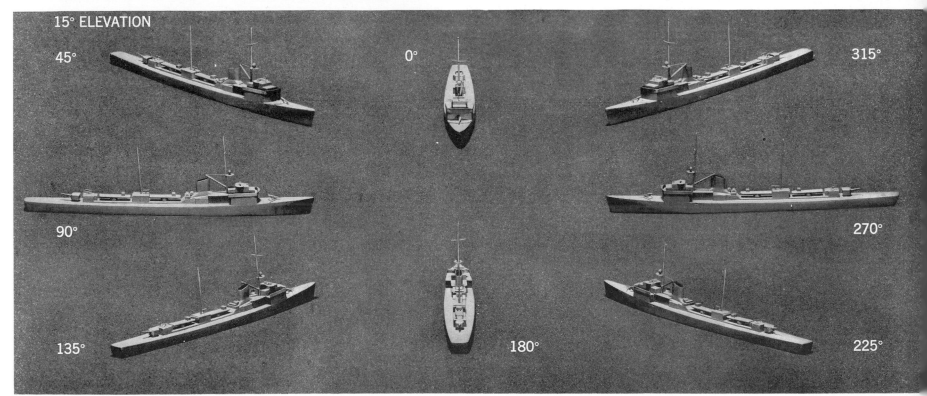

15° ELEVATION

45°

0°

315°

90°

270°

135°

180°

225°

45°

0°

315°

90°

270°

135°

180°

225°

T1 CLASS—TB 13-31

DIVISION OF NAVAL INTELLIGENCE—IDENTIFICATION AND CHARACTERISTICS SECTION—AUGUST, 1942

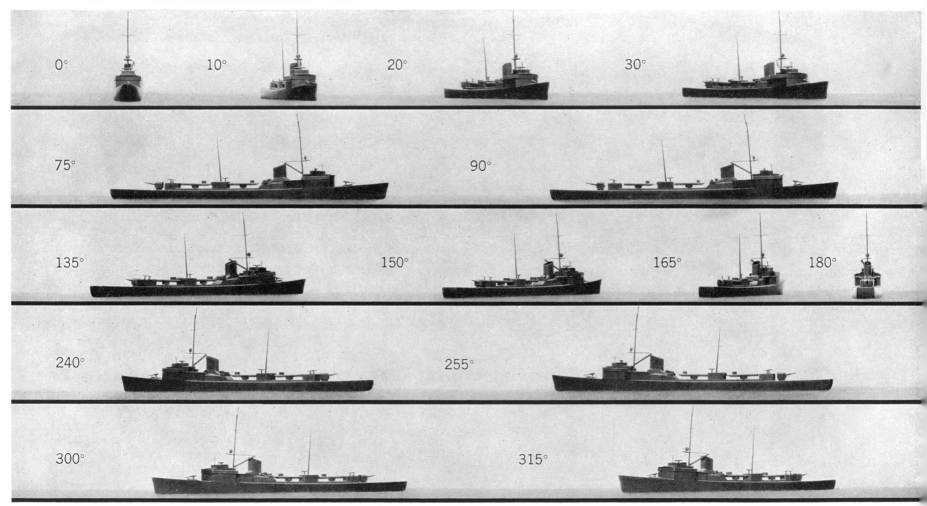

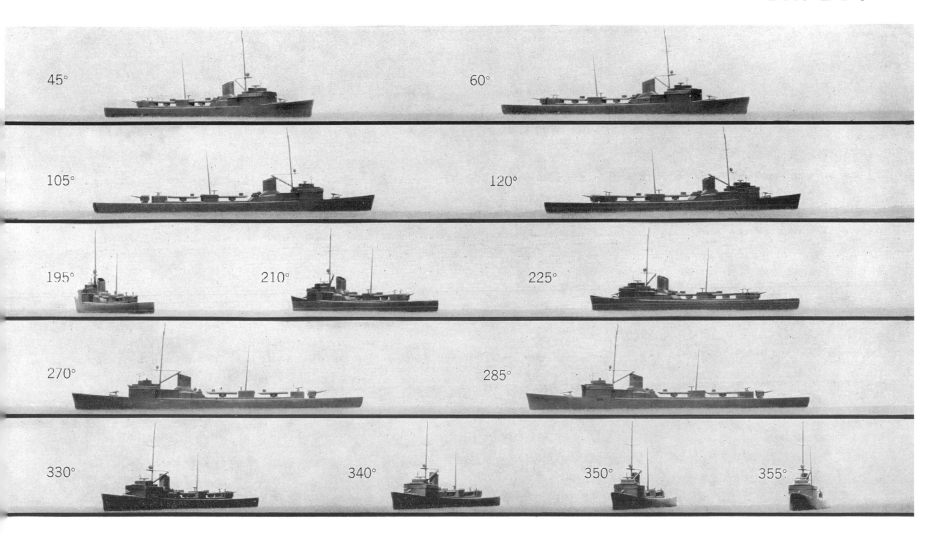

T1 CLASS TB—13-31

DIVISION OF NAVAL INTELLIGENCE—IDENTIFICATION AND CHARACTERISTICS SECTION·—AUGUST, 1942

BEGUN–1936. COMPLETED–1938-1940
SISTER SHIPS TB–T1–T19   TB 32–42 BELIEVED SIMILAR

ONI 204

RESTRICTED

1941

ONI 204 RESTRICTED

ARMAMENT

MAX. ELEV.   RANGE

3–3"9
1–1"57 AA
2 MG
2–21" TORPEDO TUBES (TWIN)
4–21" TORPEDO TUBES (TWINS) ON GYLLER ONLY
MAY CARRY LIMITED MINE LOAD

PROPULSION

DESIGNED HP   —12,500
DESIGNED SPEED—30 KTS
ENDURANCE   —1,000 AT 15 KNOTS

LENGTH 236'6" OA—232' WL
BEAM   —25'5"
DRAFT   —6'10"
        (MEAN)

DISPLACEMENT—
625 TONS (STANDARD)

HEIGHT OF OBSERVER

HORIZON BEYOND THE SHIP

SHIP BEYOND THE HORIZON

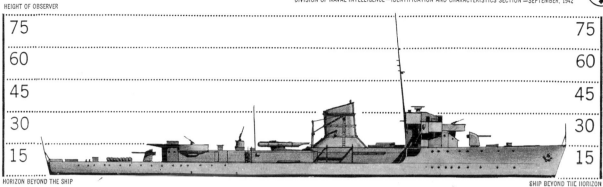

1940

1937

EX-NORWEGIAN—TB43-46

DIVISION OF NAVAL INTELLIGENCE—IDENTIFICATION AND CHARACTERISTICS SECTION—SEPTEMBER, 1942

SEIZED—APRIL, 1942

SISTER SHIPS	BEGUN	COMPLETED			
EX-ODIN— TB43	1937	1/ /40	EX-TOR— TB-45	11/ /38	/ /40
EX-BALDER—TB44 11/ /38		/ /40	EX-GYLLER—TB46	1936	7/1 /39

ONI 204
RESTRICTED

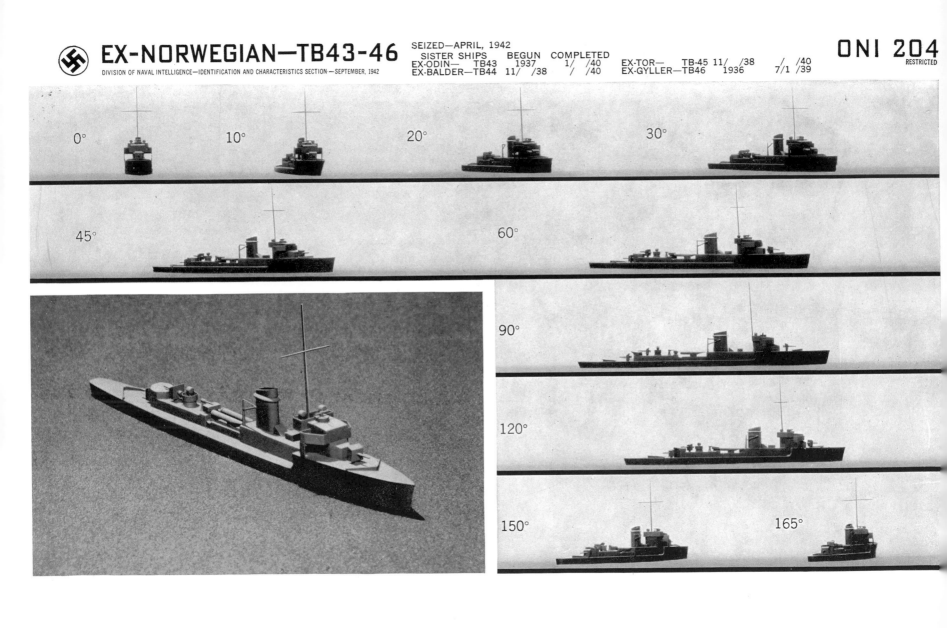

0°   10°   20°   30°   45°   60°   90°   120°   150°   165°

ARMAMENT   MAX. ELEV. RANGE

1–4"1 45 CAL.
2 AA MG
3–21", 1–19"7 TORPEDO TUBES

PROPULSION

DESIGNED H. P. —16,000
DESIGNED SPEED—31 KNOTS (NOW
             ABOUT 25 KNOTS)
ENDURANCE   —1,620 AT 15 KNOTS

NOTES

ATTACHED TO TORPEDO SCHOOL
POSSIBLE EMPLOYMENT
ESCORT AND PATROL
DUTY IN BALTIC

SISTER SHIPS	BEGUN	COMPLETED
T107—OTB 1	1911	4/30/12
T108—OTB 2	1911	8/ 6/12
T110—OTB 3	1911	7/ 1/12
T111—OTB 4	1911	8/ 8/12

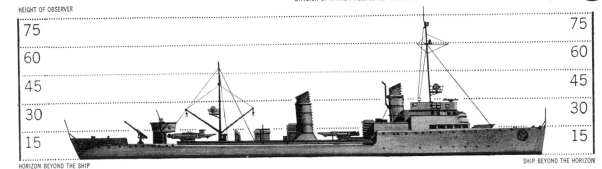

HEIGHT OF OBSERVER

HORIZON BEYOND THE SHIP

SHIP BEYOND THE HORIZON

LENGTH—256' OA—247' 8" WL
BEAM— 25'
DRAFT— 10' 6" (MAX.)

DISPLACEMENT 760 TONS
      (NORMAL)

ARMAMENT

3–4"1
2–1"46 A.A.
4 M.G.

PROPULSION

DESIGNED H.P.—8,000
DESIGNED SPEED—20 KNOTS
MACHINERY—GEARED TURBINES

NOTES

BEGUN—JUNE, 1934
COMPLETED—MAY 20, 1935
OFFICIAL DESIGNATION **AVISO**
EMPLOYMENT—
ESCORT DUTIES—TRAINING VESSEL

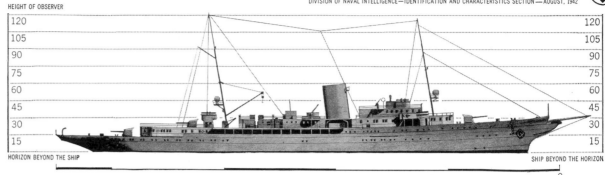

HEIGHT OF OBSERVER

HORIZON BEYOND THE SHIP

SHIP BEYOND THE HORIZON

LENGTH—377' 4" OA
BEAM— 44' 4"
DRAFT— 11' 3"

DISPLACEMENT—2,560 TONS
(STANDARD)

AUG. 1936

740 TON

517 TON

250 TON

740 TON—OCEANGOING

DIMENSIONS—	244½′X20½′X13½′
ARMAMENT—	1—4".1 2-.79"AA
TORPEDO TUBES—	6-21"(4 BOW 2 STERN)
MAX SPEED—	18⅜KTS-ENDURANCE 14000 MI
COMPLEMENT—	40

517 TON—SEAGOING

DIMENSIONS—	206–213′X20′X13′
ARMAMENT—	1—3".5 1-.79"AA
TORPEDO TUBES—	5-21" (4 BOW 1 STERN)
MAX SPEED—	16⅝ KTS-ENDURANCE 10,000 MI
COMPLEMENT—	35

250 TON—COASTAL

DIMENSIONS—	136½′X13′X12¾′
ARMAMENT—	1-.79"AA
TORPEDO TUBES—	3-21" (BOW)
MAX SPEED—	13 KNOTS-ENDURANCE 3000 MI
COMPLEMENT—	23

SEIZURES—UA EX-TURKISH BATIRAY 1028 TONS   UB EX-BRITISH SEAL 1500 TONS   EX-DUTCH 0-25, 26, 27, 888 TONS

TACTICAL VIEWS

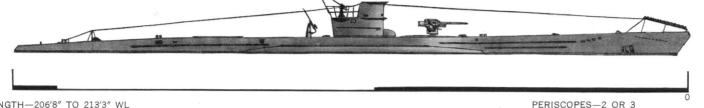

LENGTH—206'8" TO 213'3" WL
BEAM —19' TO 19'8" (EXTREME)

PERISCOPES—2 OR 3
THIN—   23' ABOVE CT LID
THICK—   14' ABOVE CT LID

DISPLACEMENT—517 TONS (STANDARD) SURFACE

KNOTS	RPM
16	480
15.5	460
15.1	440
14.6	420
13.8	400
12.9	380
12	360
11.25	340
10.6	320
10	300
9.5	280
9	260
8.6	240
8.1	220
7.5	200
6.9	180
6.2	160
5.25	140

ARMAMENT

1–3"5
1–20mm
REMOVABLE AAMG MAY BE AFT OF CT
TORPEDO TUBES–4 BOW–1 STERN
TORPEDOES–533mm–30 KTS 5400 YDS
CAPABLE OF DISCHARGING MINES THROUGH
TORPEDO TUBES

PROPULSION

MACHINERY   —2 1400 HP, 6 CYLINDER, 4 STROKE MAN DIESEL
BATTERIES   —
FUEL   —OIL—31,670 GALS.
DESIGNED HP —2,000 (SURFACE)
DESIGNED SPEED—18 KTS (SURFACE) 8 KTS (SUBMERGED)
ENDURANCE   —10,000 @ 10 KTS
              100 @ 8 KTS (SUBMERGED)

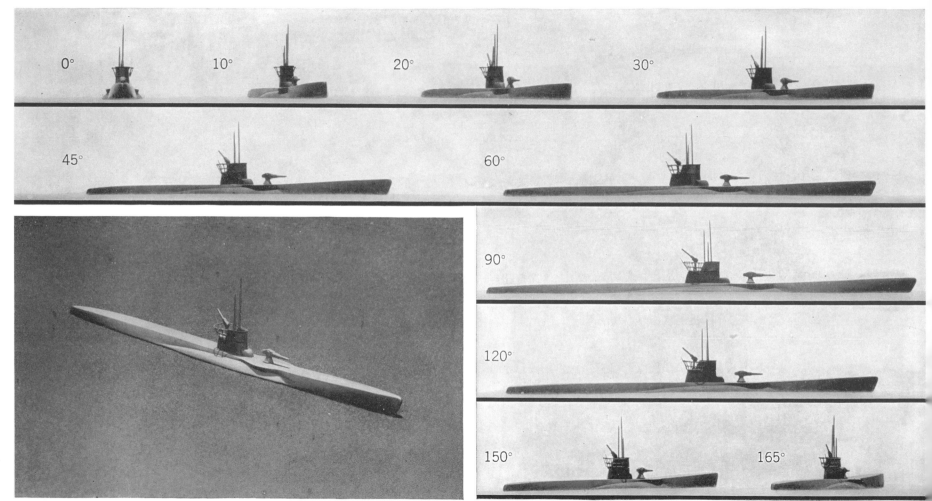

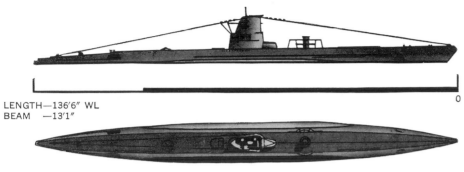

LENGTH—136'6" WL
BEAM   —13'1"

DISPLACEMENT—250 TONS (STANDARD)

ARMAMENT

LIGHT AA GUN (REMOVABLE)
3–21" TORPEDO TUBES (BOW)
CAPABLE OF DISCHARGING MINES THROUGH
TORPEDO TUBES

KNOTS	RPM
13	165
	120
	400
	350
	300
	275
	250
	245
	240
	220
	200
	160
	150
	120
3	100
	80

PROPULSION

MACHINERY   —2–350 HP, 4 CYCLE, SINGLE ACTING DIESELS
               2 ELECTRIC MOTORS
DESIGNED HP   —700 (SURFACE)—360 (SUBMERGED)
DESIGNED SPEED—13 (SURFACE)— 7 (SUBMERGED)
ENDURANCE   —4,000 @ 10 KNOTS
               50 @ 4 KNOTS (SUBMERGED)

NOTES

USED ENTIRELY FOR COASTAL OPERATION

500 TON CLASS SS

NOTE: STERN DECK TORPEDO TUBE

300 **TON CLASS SS**

DIMENSIONS—
LENGTH—130′

DISPLACEMENT—
290 TONS (SURFACE)
310 TONS (SUBMERGED)

ARMAMENT—
SOME HAVE LIGHT AA GUNS OR 1 OR
2 MG

PROPULSION—
MAXIMUM SPEED—16–20 KTS (SURFACE)
8–10 KTS (SUB-
MERGED)
ENDURANCE   —60 DAYS AT SEA
SIMILAR TO 250 TON CLASS WITH SADDLE TANKS ADDED

500 **TON CLASS SS**

DESIGN—
SIMILAR IN APPEARANCE TO THAT OF
517 TON CLASS.

MOST OF THIS CLASS SUNK.
REMAINDER REPORTED BEING USED
FOR TRAINING PURPOSES

1060 **TON CLASS SS**

DIMENSIONS—
LENGTH—260′–275′7″ WL
BEAM   —20′6″

DISPLACEMENT—
1060 TONS (STANDARD)

ARMAMENT—
1–4″1 45 CAL (FORWARD)
CAPABLE OF LAYING MINES THROUGH
TORPEDO TUBES

PROPULSION—
DESIGNED HP—3,200
ENDURANCE   —7,000–8,000 (SURFACE)

ONI 204 RESTRICTED

ARMAMENT

2-4″1 GUN SHIELDS
1-1″46
2 MG

 MAX. ELEV. RANGE

PROPULSION

DESIGNED H.P.—2,600
DESIGNED SPEED—17 KTS

KNOTS	R.P.M.
	420
	400
	350
	300
	275
	250
	245
	240
	220
	200
	160
	150
	120
	80

HEIGHT OF OBSERVER

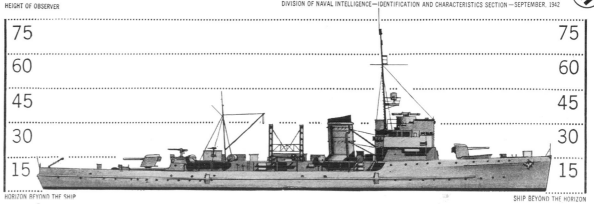

75 — 75
60 — 60
45 — 45
30 — 30
15 — 15

HORIZON BEYOND THE SHIP SHIP BEYOND THE HORIZON

0

LENGTH—216′ 6″ OA
BEAM —27′ 3″
DRAFT — 6′ 1″ (MEAN)

DISPLACEMENT—600 TONS
(STANDARD)

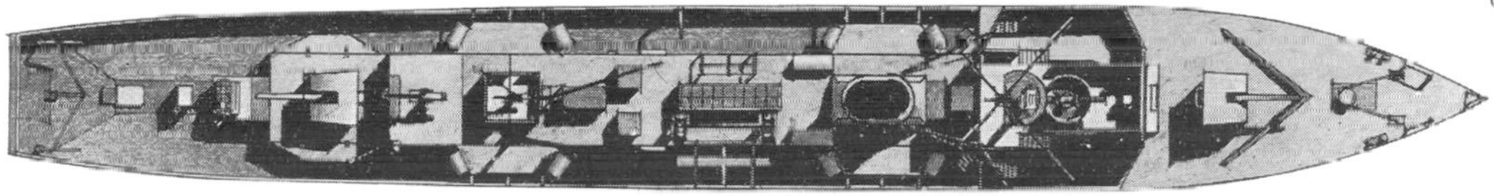

1939

1939

M-1 CLASS—AM27-66
DIVISION OF NAVAL INTELLIGENCE—IDENTIFICATION AND CHARACTERISTICS SECTION—SEPTEMBER, 1942

SISTER SHIPS
M 1-40

BEGUN
1936

COMPLETED
1938–1941

A NUMBER OF THESE HAVE BEEN LOST, IDENTITY NOT ESTABLISHED

ONI 204

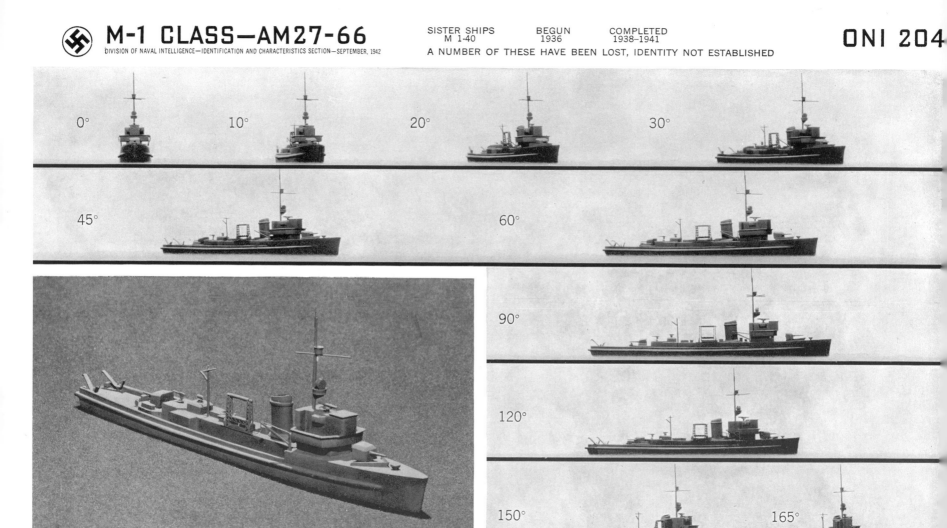

0° 10° 20° 30° 45° 60° 90° 120° 150° 165°

ONI 204

LENGTH—106   BEAM—16'   DRAFT—5'
DISPLACEMENT—85 TONS (FULL LOAD)
DES HP—2,700
SPEED—33-34½ KNOTS (MAX)
ENDURANCE—500 @ 30 KNOTS

ARMAMENT—2-1″46
           1- ″78
           2 21″ TORPEDO TUBES

TWO OTHER TYPES

	A	B
LENGTH—	92'	115'
BEAM—	13'6″	16'6″
DRAFT—	5'	5'6″
DISPLACEMENT—	63 TONS	
TORPEDO TUBES—	2-21″	2-21″, 6 MINES
ARMAMENT—	1-″79, 1-″51	2-″79, 2-″311 MG
DES HP—		6000
SPEED—	33 KNOTS	35 KNOTS
ENDURANCE—	500 @ 30 KTS	600 @ 32 KTS

B—SPEED TABLE

KNOTS	RPM	KNOTS	RPM
35	1520	24	1120
33	1440	22	1040
31	1370	20	960
28	1250	15	700

NEW TYPE

EARLY SERIES ↓

LENGTH—	85'–121'5"
BEAM—	14'6"
DRAFT—	4'10"
DISPLACEMENT—	44–90 TONS
DES HP—	700–1800
SPEED—	17–18 KNOTS

ARMAMENT—1 OR 2–.79 AA

DIVISION OF NAVAL INTELLIGENCE—IDENTIFICATION AND CHARACTERISTICS SECTION—OCTOBER, 1942

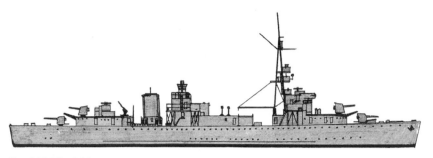

Ex-GRYF—CM 1   ex-**POLISH**

COMPLETED	—FEBRUARY 27, 1938
DIMENSIONS	—323'8" WL X 42'10" X 11'8" (MEAN)
DISPLACEMENT	—2,085 TONS (STANDARD)
ARMAMENT	—6-4".7; 4-1"57 AA
	TORPEDO TUBES—1; 200 MINES
PROPULSION	—HP—6,000 (DES)
	SPEED—20.6 KNOTS (DES)

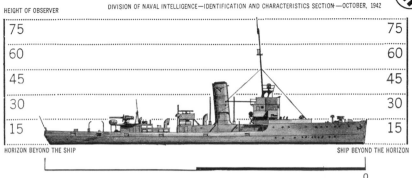

HEIGHT OF OBSERVER

HORIZON BEYOND THE SHIP   SHIP BEYOND THE HORIZON

DIMENSIONS—184'1"–189'8" WL X 23'11"–27'1"
X 7'3" (MAXIMUM), 6'4"–6'6" (MEAN)

M-60 CLASS   **AM-1 TO 26**

LAUNCHED	—1917-18
COMPLETED	—1917-18-19
DISPLACEMENT	—414-455 TONS (STANDARD)
ARMAMENT	—1-4".1; 1 MG
PROPULSION	—HP—1,800 (DES)
	SPEED—16 KNOTS (DES)
	ENDURANCE—1,830 @ 10 KNOTS

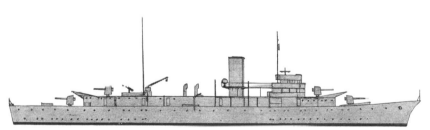

ALBATROS (ex-OLAV TRYGGVASON)—CM 2   ex-**NORWEGIAN**

COMPLETED	—MAY 18, 1934
DIMENSIONS	—319'3" X 37'7" X 11'7" (MAXIMUM)
DISPLACEMENT	—1,747 TONS (NORMAL)
ARMAMENT	—4-4".7; 1-3" AA; 2-1".5;
	TORPEDO TUBES—2-17".7; 280 MINES
PROPULSION	—HP—6,000 (DES)
	SPEED—20 KNOTS (DES)
	ENDURANCE—3,000 @ 14 KNOTS

LAUGEN, GLOMMEN—CM   ex-**NORWEGIAN**

COMPLETED	—1917
DISPLACEMENT	—335 TONS

REPORTED USED AS PATROL VESSELS

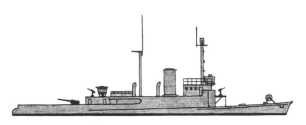

WILLEM VAN EWIJCK—AM 72
PIETER FLORISZ—AM 73
ABRAHAM VAN DER HULST—AM 74

ex-DUTCH

COMPLETED—1937
DIMENSIONS—184'4" X 25'7" X 7'10½" (MEAN)
DISPLACEMENT—460 TONS (STANDARD)
ARMAMENT—1–3"; 4–0".46 MG; 16 MINES
PROPULSION—HP 1,600 (DES.)
SPEED—15.5 KNOTS (DES.)

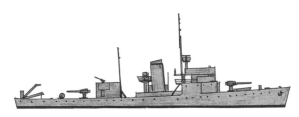

SÖLÖVEN—AM 69

ex-DANISH

COMPLETED—JUNE 8, 1939
DIMENSIONS—175'8" X 20'8" X 6'5" (MAXIMUM)
DISPLACEMENT—270 TONS (STANDARD)
ARMAMENT—2–2".95; 4–0".78; 4 MG; 2 DC RELEASE GEARS; 30 MINES
PROPULSION—HP 2,200 (DES.)
SPEED—18 KNOTS (DES.)

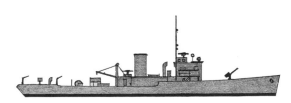

OTRA—AM 70, RAUMA—AM 71

ex-NORWEGIAN

COMPLETED—1940
DIMENSIONS—168'4" X 23'2" X 5'11" (MEAN)
DISPLACEMENT—360 TONS (STANDARD)
ARMAMENT—1–1".57; 2–0".5 MG
PROPULSION—HP 900 (DES.)
SPEED—13.5 KNOTS (DES.)
ENDURANCE—1,400 @ 9 KNOTS

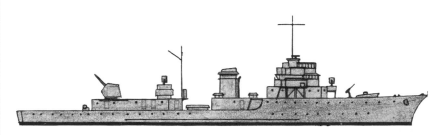

ELAN CLASS—AM 75
NUMBER UNDETERMINED

ex-FRENCH

COMPLETED—1939–40
DIMENSIONS—254'3" X 27'11" X 7'10" (MEAN)
DISPLACEMENT—647 TONS (STANDARD)
ARMAMENT—2–3".9 AA; 8 AA MG
PROPULSION—HP 4,000 (DES.)
SPEED—20 KNOTS (DES.)

ARMAMENT— UNKNOWN

DESIGNED HP— 5,800

DESIGNED SPEED—16 KNOTS

AIRCRAFT— 2 FLOATPLANES
1 CATAPULT

LENGTH—455′

BEAM— 54′1″

DRAFT— 19′9″ (MAX)

COMPLETED—1937

DISPLACEMENT—5,434 TONS (GROSS)

HEIGHT OF OBSERVER

135		135
120		120
105		105
90		90
75		75
60		60
45		45
30		30
15		15

HORIZON BEYOND THE SHIP

SHIP BEYOND THE HORIZON

0

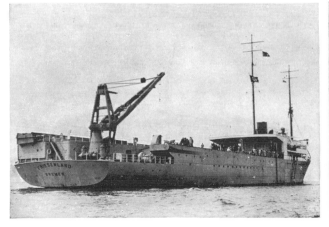

3/22/39

WESTFALEN—AVC 1   1906

DISPLACEMENT—5,365 TONS (GROSS)

LENGTH—   409' OA   BEAM—53'

DESIGNED HP— 2,200 (APPROX)   DESIGNED SPEED—11.5 KNOTS

AIRCRAFT—   1 CATAPULT—2 SEAPLANE SCOUTS

SCHWABENLAND—AVC 2   1925

DISPLACEMENT—8,188 TONS (GROSS)

LENGTH—   468'2" OA   BEAM—60'4"   DRAFT—27'9" (FULL LOAD)

DESIGNED HP— 3,600   DESIGNED SPEED—12 KNOTS

AIRCRAFT—   1 CATAPULT—2 SEAPLANE SCOUTS

OSTMARK—AVC 3   1936

DISPLACEMENT—   1,280 TONS (GROSS)

LENGTH—   242'8" OA

BEAM—   37'

DRAFT—   13'1" (FULL LOAD)

DESIGNED HP—   2,000

DESIGNED SPEED— 13.5 KNOTS

HEIGHT OF OBSERVER

90	90
75	75
60	60
45	45
30	30
15	15

HORIZON BEYOND THE SHIP

SHIP BEYOND THE HORIZON

0

LENGTH 249'– 4" OA—241'–1" WL
BEAM 28'–10"
DRAFT 6'– 1" (MEAN)

DISPLACEMENT–600 TONS

ARMAMENT

2–4"1 50 CAL   MAX. EL–80°
4–1"46 AA
2–M.G.
D.C. THROWERS
EQUIPPED FOR MINELAYING

PROPULSION

BOILERS–   4–H.P. WATER TUBE
FUEL–   OIL 245 TONS
DESIGNED H.P.–   13,500
DESIGNED SPEED–28 KTS
ENDURANCE–   1600 AT 20 KTS

KÖNIGIN LUISE—F-3

F-1 CLASS—PG1-10

DIVISION OF NAVAL INTELLIGENCE—IDENTIFICATION AND CHARACTERISTICS SECTION—AUGUST, 1942

KÖNIGIN
LUISE

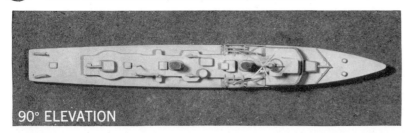

90° ELEVATION

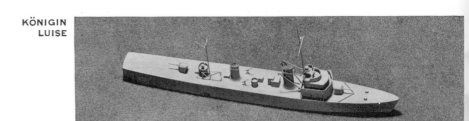

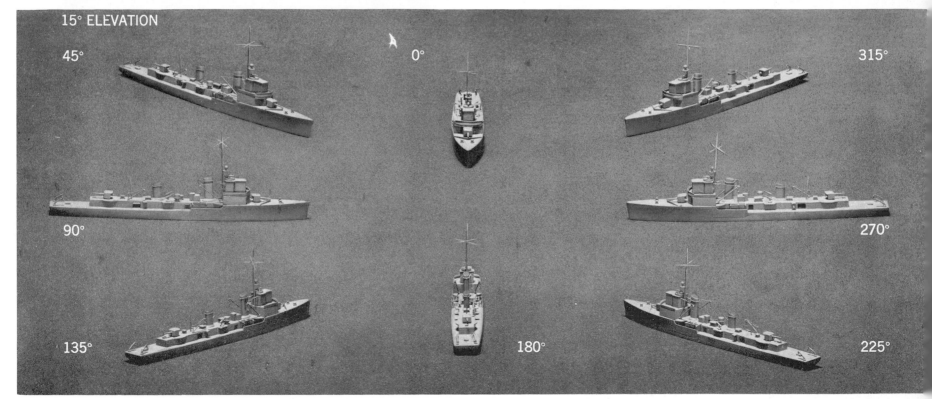

15° ELEVATION

45°

0°

315°

90°

270°

135°

180°

225°

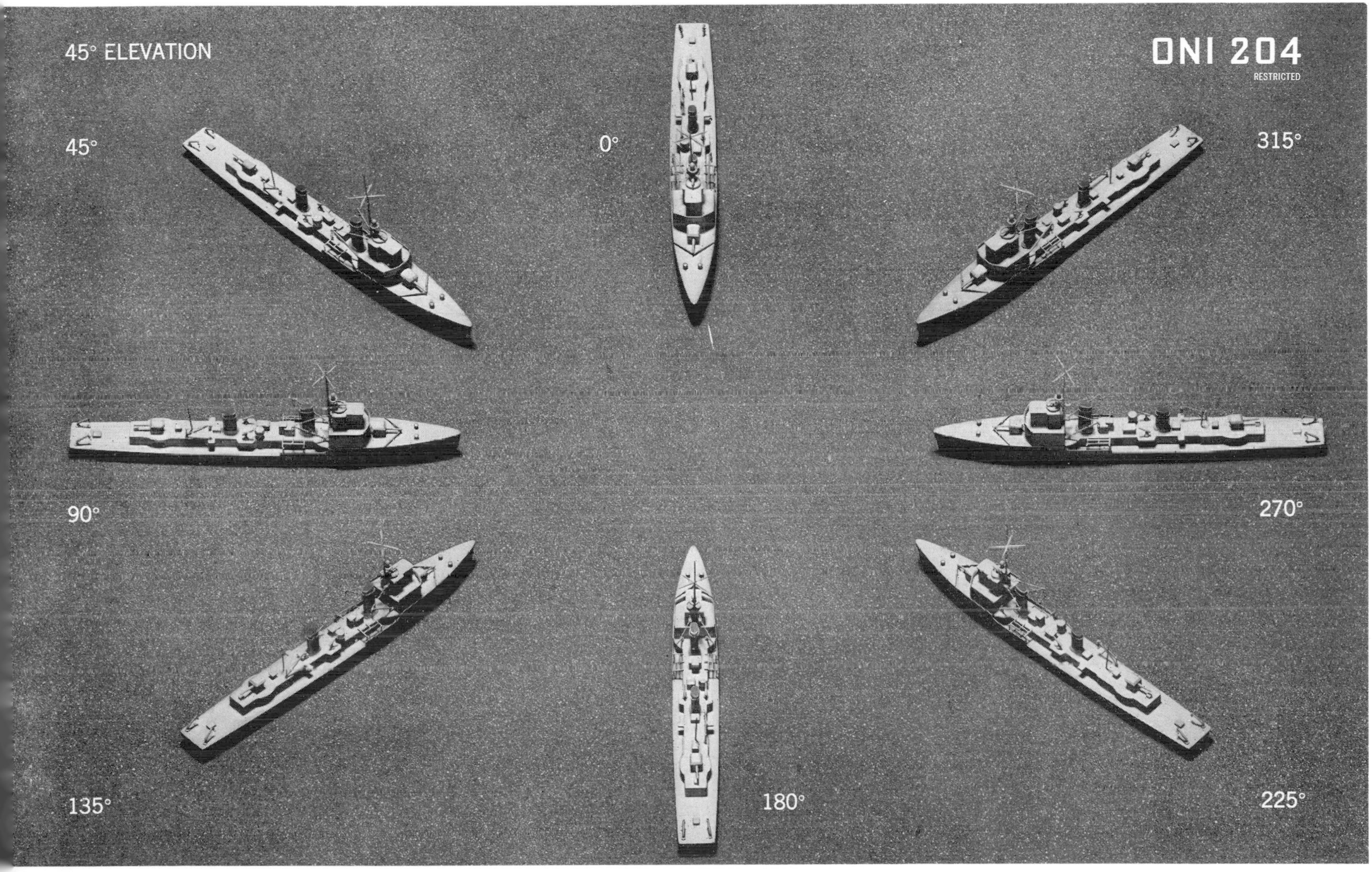

45°

0°

315°

90°

270°

135°

180°

225°

F-1 CLASS—PG1-10

DIVISION OF NAVAL INTELLIGENCE—IDENTIFICATION AND CHARACTERISTICS SECTION—AUGUST, 1942

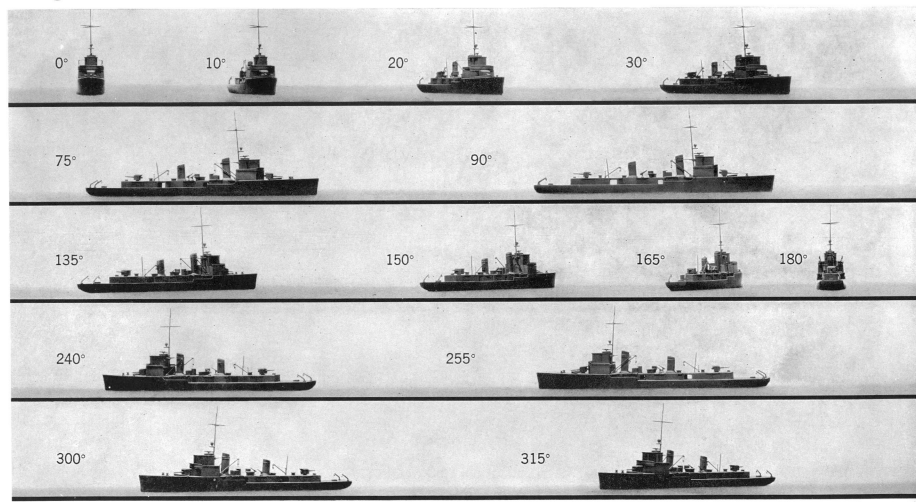

0° 10° 20° 30°

75° 90°

135° 150° 165° 180°

240° 255°

300° 315°

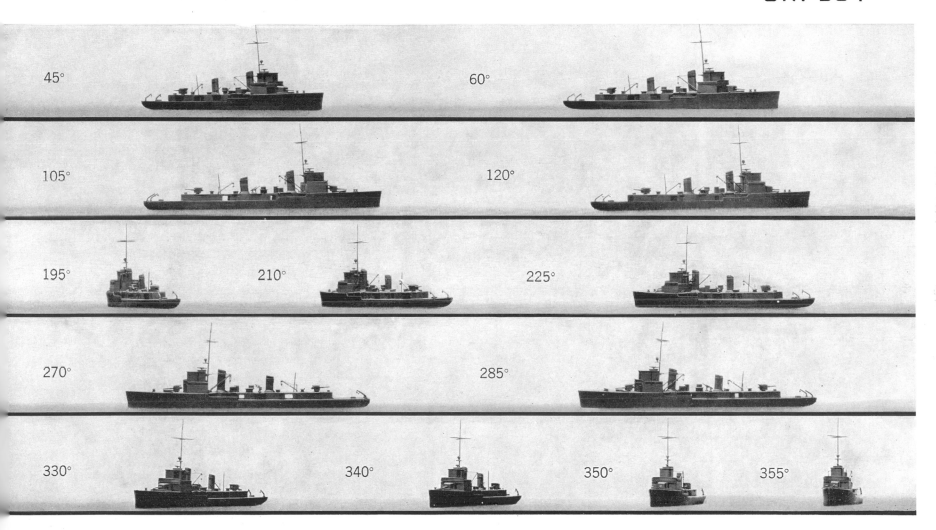

45°

60°

105°

120°

195°

210°

225°

270°

285°

330°

340°

350°

355°

F-1 CLASS—PG1-10

DIVISION OF NAVAL INTELLIGENCE—IDENTIFICATION AND CHARACTERISTICS SECTION —AUGUST, 1942

BEGUN–1934-'35 COMPLETED–1935, F-10 IN 4/'38   ALL PHOTOS TAKEN–1938

CLASS–F1, F-2, KÖNIGIN LUISE, F-4, F-5, HAI, F-7, F-8, F-9, F-10

ONI 204

RESTRICTED

AFT STACK SINCE LOWERED. MAINMAST STRUCK

ARMAMENT

4-4".1 AA
2-3".5 AA
4-1".5 AA
ARMAMENT VARIABLE

PROTECTION

LIGHT WEATHER SHIELDS TO MOUNTS

KTS.	R.P.M.
	420
	400
	350
	300
	275
	250
	245
	240
	220
	200
	160
	150
	120
	80

DES. H.P. —7000
DES. SPD.—20 KTS.

LENGTH—370'9" OA—354'4" WL
BEAM —44'6"
DRAFT —13'1" (MAXIMUM)
        11'6" (MEAN)

DISPLACEMENT
2,410 TONS (STANDARD)

HEIGHT OF OBSERVER

105 / 105
90 / 90
75 / 75
60 / 60
45 / 45
30 / 30
15 / 15

HORIZON BEYOND THE SHIP

SHIP BEYOND THE HORIZON

0

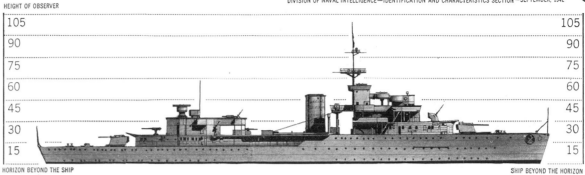

T-155—6/25/08   **T-157**—8/27/08
T-156—7/21/08   **T-158**—10/8/08

DISPLACEMENT—664 TONS (NORMAL)
LENGTH— 236'7" OA
BEAM— 25'7"
DRAFT— 10'2" (MAXIMUM)
DES HP— 10,800
DES SPD— 22 KTS
ARMAMENT— 1 AAMG (T-158—1-3"4)
2–19"7 TT

EQUIPPED FOR MINE LAYING

BLITZ   1907

DISPLACEMENT—650 TONS (NORMAL)
LENGTH— 231' OA
BEAM— 25'7"
DRAFT— 8'10" (MAX)
DES HP— 10,000
DES SPD— 30 KTS

PFEIL   1907

DISPLACEMENT—650 TONS (NORMAL)
LENGTH— 231' OA
BEAM— 25'7"
DRAFT— 8'10" (MAX)
DES HP— 10,000
DES SPD— 30 KTS

EDUARD JUNGMANN   5/9/08

DISPLACEMENT—664 TONS (NORMAL)
LENGTH— 236'7" OA
BEAM— 25'7"
DRAFT— 10'2" (MAX)
DES HP— 10,800
DES SPD— 30 KTS
ARMAMENT— 2–3"4
2–19"7 TT

KLAUS VON BEVERN   COMPLETED 8/5/11

DISPLACEMENT—787 TONS (NORMAL)
LENGTH— 242'10" OA
BEAM— 25'11"
DRAFT— 10'6" (MAXIMUM)
DES HP— 18,000
DES SPD— 29 KTS
ARMAMENT— 2–4"1
2–19"7 TORPEDO TUBES

KOMET   2/29/08

DISPLACEMENT—664 TONS (NORMAL)
LENGTH— 236'7" OA
BEAM— 25'7"
DRAFT— 10'2" (MAXIMUM)
DES HP— 10,080
DES SPD— 30 KTS
ARMAMENT— 2–3"5
2–19"7 TORPEDO TUBES
EQUIPPED TO CARRY MINES

T-196 (EX-MINE SWEEPER LEADER)   11/10/11

DISPLACEMENT—787 TONS (NORMAL)
LENGTH— 242'10" OA
BEAM— 25'11"
DRAFT— 10'6" (MAXIMUM)
DES HP— 18,000
DES SPD— 29 KNOTS
ARMAMENT— 2–4"1
2–19"7 TORPEDO TUBES

T-123   11/1/13

DISPLACEMENT—630 TONS (NORMAL)
LENGTH— 234'7" OA
BEAM— 24'4"
DRAFT— 10' (MAXIMUM)
DES HP— 15,700
DES SPD— 22 KTS
ARMAMENT— 2 AAMG
EQUIPPED FOR MINE LAYING

LENGTH—154'

BEAM— 21'4"

DRAFT— 4'4" (MAX)

DISPLACEMENT—320 TONS (STANDARD)

LOAD— 120 TONS (4-7 TANKS)

ARMAMENT— 1-3", 2-8 MG

PROTECTION— .79" PLATE—WHEELHOUSE

PROPULSION— 3 DIESELS—390 HP

SPEED— 12 KNOTS (MAX)

OTHER TYPES REPORTED

A DIMENSIONS— 98'5"X26'3"X27½"

    CAPACITY— 20 TONS

    POWER— 2-75 HP DIESEL

    SPEED— 10.5 KNOTS

B DIMENSIONS— 65-82'X16-20', 6 KNOTS

C CONCRETE BARGES

    DIMENSIONS— 180-200' LONG

    CAPACITY—300 TONS (2-25-TON TANKS, 1000 MEN)

D 1000-TON TLC OVER 390' LONG

KRISCHAN I   1935

DISPLACEMENT— 200 TONS (STANDARD)
LENGTH— 121'6" OA
BEAM— 22'8"
DRAFT— 8'3" (MAXIMUM)
DESIGNED HP— 800
DESIGNED SPEED—?15 KNOTS

GUNTHER VON PLUSCHOU   1935

DISPLACEMENT— 450 TONS (STANDARD)
LENGTH— 166'4" OA
BEAM— 26'4"

BERNHARD VON TSCHIERSCHKI   1935

DISPLACEMENT— 800 TONS (STANDARD)
LENGTH— 249'1"
BEAM— 36'1"

SCHLENDERPRAHM   8/25/38

DISPLACEMENT— OVER 1,000 TONS (STANDARD)

GREIF   1936

DISPLACEMENT— 950 TONS (STANDARD)
LENGTH— 236'3" OA
BEAM— 34'8"
DRAFT— 9'6"
DESIGNED HP— 4,400
DESIGNED SPEED—19 KNOTS

HANS ROLSHOVEN   1937

DISPLACEMENT— 935 TONS (STANDARD)
LENGTH— 249'5"
BEAM— 34'8"
DRAFT— 11'2" (MAXIMUM)
DESIGNED HP— 7,200
DESIGNED SPEED—22 KNOTS

WILHELM GUSTLOFF   1937

DISPLACEMENT—   25,484 TONS (GROSS)
DESIGNED HP—   9,500
DESIGNED SPEED—16 KNOTS

GLUCKAUF   1913

DISPLACEMENT—   1,915 TONS (GROSS)
DESIGNED HP—   1,300
DESIGNED SPEED—12 KNOTS

METEOR   1904

DISPLACEMENT—   5,717 TONS (GROSS)
DESIGNED SPEED—12 KNOTS

ROBERT LEY   1938

DISPLACEMENT—   27,288 TONS
LENGTH—   635'5"
BEAM—   79'
DRAFT—   45'

RÜGEN   1915

DISPLACEMENT—   2,074 TONS (GROSS)
DESIGNED HP—   3,200
DESIGNED SPEED—15 KNOTS

OBERHAUSEN   1939

DISPLACEMENT—   1,261 TONS (GROSS)
DESIGNED SPEED—?15 KNOTS

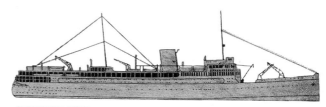

BERLIN   1935

DISPLACEMENT—   15,286 TONS (GROSS)
DESIGNED HP—   12,000
DESIGNED SPEED—16.5 KNOTS

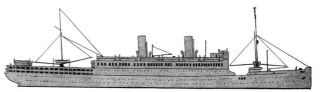

STUTTGART   1923

DISPLACEMENT—   13,387 TONS (GROSS)
DESIGNED HP—   8,500
DESIGNED SPEED—16 KNOTS

STRASSBURG   1930

DISPLACEMENT—   17,000 TONS (GROSS)
DESIGNED SPEED—18.5 KNOTS

HECHT   1918

DISPLACEMENT—448 TONS (STANDARD)
LENGTH— 189'8" WL   BEAM—23'11"   DRAFT—6'6" (MEAN)
DESIGNED HP— 1,800   DESIGNED SPEED—16 KNOTS
ENDURANCE— 1,830 MILES AT 10 KNOTS
ARMAMENT— 1-4"1—1 AAMG
OTHERS SIMILAR WITH MINOR VARIATIONS—JAGD, DELPHIN, ACHERON, FRAUENLOB, GAZELLE, HAVEL—1917-1919

STÖRTEBEKER   1918

DISPLACEMENT—448 TONS (STANDARD)
LENGTH—   193' OA—189'8" WL   BEAM—23'11"   DRAFT—6'6"(MEAN)
DESIGNED HP   1,800   DESIGNED SPEED—16 KNOTS
ENDURANCE—   1,830 MILES AT 10 KNOTS
ARMAMENT—   1-4"1—1 AAMG

PELIKAN, NAUTILUS—(EXPERIMENTAL BARRAGE VESSELS)   1918

DISPLACEMENT—492 TONS (NORMAL)

LENGTH—   193' OA   BEAM—23'11"   DRAFT—8'6" (MAXIMUM)

DESIGNED HP—   1,800 DESIGNED SPEED—17 KNOTS

ENDURANCE—   1,830 MILES AT 10 KNOTS

BROMMY   1916

DISPLACEMENT—384 TONS (STANDARD)
LENGTH—   187' WL   BEAM—23'11"   DRAFT—3'7" (MEAN)
DESIGNED HP— 1,800   DESIGNED SPEED—16 KNOTS
ENDURANCE—   1,830 AT 10 KNOTS   ARMAMENT—1-4"1   1 AAMG
FUCHS, TOKU, RAULE, VON DER GROEBEN, ARKONA, SÜNDEWALL—MINOR VARIATIONS

DAHME 1936

DISPLACEMENT—	475 TONS
LENGTH—	186'
BEAM—	26'3"
DRAFT—	13'

STRAHL 1902

DISPLACEMENT—	1,121 TONS (NORMAL)		
LENGTH—	235'	BEAM—	33'6"
DRAFT—	11'4"		
DESIGNED HP—	800	DESIGNED SPEED—10 KNOTS	

PREGEL 1936

DISPLACEMENT—	186 TONS
LENGTH—	114'6"
BEAM—	21'4"
DRAFT—	7'2"

SPREE 1938

DISPLACEMENT—	222 TONS
LENGTH—	127'
BEAM—	21'4"
DRAFT—	8'2"

NOGAT 1937

DISPLACEMENT—	186 TONS	LENGTH—	126'2"
BEAM—	21'5"	DRAFT—	7'6"

NECK, HEISTERNEST—NO DATA

OUTPOST VESSELS (CONVERTED TRAWLERS)   **40 ANTI-SUBMARINE**
108 IN NUMBER —?-3" OR 4"1 AA, ?-0"79 OR 1"46 AA   **CRAFT**—NO DATA
  24 IN NUMBER —?-4"1 AA   ABOUT 70 MORE—DETAILS UNKNOWN

ST. LOUIS   1929

DISPLACEMENT—16,732 TONS (GROSS)
LENGTH   543'8" OA
BEAM—   60'8"
DRAFT—   32'
DESIGNED HP— 12,000

IBERIA image and data:

IBERIA   1928

DISPLACEMENT—9,829 TONS (GROSS)
LENGTH—   485'9" OA
BEAM—   60'8"
DRAFT—   34'6" (MAXIMUM)
DESIGNED HP— 8,000

ERWIN WASSNER   1929

DISPLACEMENT—   5,170 TONS

DESIGNED HP—   6,500

DESIGNED SPEED—18 KNOTS

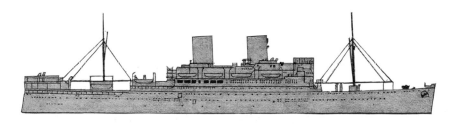

PRETORIA   1936

DISPLACEMENT—16,662 TONS (GROSS)
LENGTH—   547'8" OA
BEAM—   72'5"
DRAFT—   31'5" (MAXIMUM)

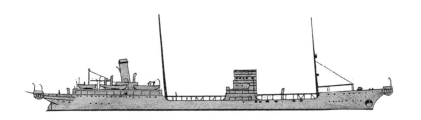

NEPTUN   1926

DISPLACEMENT—7,250 TONS (GROSS)
LENGTH—   434' OA
BEAM—   57'
DRAFT—   32'

TSINGTAU   9/24/34

DISPLACEMENT—	1,970 TONS (STANDARD)
LENGTH—	287′ OA
BEAM—	44′4″
DRAFT—	13′3″
DESIGNED HP—	4,100
DESIGNED SPEED—	17.5 KNOTS
ARMAMENT—	2-3″.5 (45) AA

SAAR   1/10/34

DISPLACEMENT—	2,710 TONS (STANDARD)
LENGTH—	329′5″ OA
BEAM—	44′4″
DRAFT—	14′2″ (FULL LOAD)
DESIGNED HP—	3,700
DESIGNED SPEED—	16 KNOTS
ARMAMENT—	3-4″.1 45 CAL. 4-AAMG

TANGA   1/21/39

DISPLACEMENT—	4,200 TONS
LENGTH—	295′4″ OA
BEAM—	47′
DRAFT—	17′9″ (FULL LOAD)

WEICHSEL   1923

DISPLACEMENT—	3,974 TONS (NORMAL)
LENGTH—	331′4″ OA
BEAM—	44′1″
DRAFT—	20′
DESIGNED HP—	1,400
DESIGNED SPEED—	10.5 KNOTS
ARMAMENT—	1-?

WALDEMAR KOPHAMEL   1940

WILHELM BAUER   1940

DISPLACEMENT—2,500 TONS (STANDARD)

DESIGNED HP— 22,400

SATAN   1912

DISPLACEMENT—	1,069 TONS (GROSS)
LENGTH—	209′ OA
BEAM—	32′
DRAFT—	14′6″
DESIGNED SPEED—	13 KNOTS

ADOLPH LÜDERITZ   1940

KARL PETERS   1940

DISPLACEMENT—3,000 (APPROX.)

SFAX, HERTHA & UNIDENTIFIED CRAFT   **NO DATA**

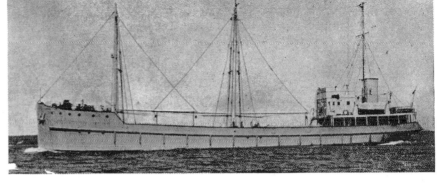

MEMEL　　　　　　　　　　　　　　1937

DISPLACEMENT— 998 TONS (NORMAL)
DESIGNED SPEED—13 KNOTS

MOSEL　　　　　　　　　　　　　　1912

DISPLACEMENT— 352 TONS (NORMAL)
DESIGNED HP— 250
DESIGNED SPEED—9 KNOTS

ISAR

DISPLACEMENT— 3,850 TONS
LENGTH— 319'
BEAM— 45'6"
DRAFT— 13'
DESIGNED HP— 2,000
DESIGNED SPEED—12 KNOTS

DONAU　　1937 (PURCHASED)

DISPLACEMENT— 3,950 TONS
　　　　　　　　(NORMAL)
LENGTH— 303'8" OA
BEAM— 41'7"
DRAFT— 17'6" (FULL LOAD)
DESIGNED SPEED—10 KNOTS

LECH　　　　　　　1930

DISPLACEMENT— 1,171 TONS (GROSS)
LENGTH— 319'1" OA
BEAM— 45'6"
DRAFT— 15'5" (MAXIMUM)
DESIGNED SPEED—13 KNOTS

WARNOW

DISPLACEMENT— 726 TONS (GROSS)
DESIGNED SPEED—13 KNOTS

ODIN　　　　　　　1912-16

DISPLACEMENT— 400 TONS (NORMAL)
LENGTH— 117-136 OA
BEAM— 22'-24'
DRAFT— 11' (FULL LOAD)
DESIGNED HP— 400
DESIGNED SPEED—10 KNOTS
ARMAMENT— 1-3".5—1 AAMG

AO—AE—AP—ACL

AO-BRÖSEN   1915

DISPLACEMENT—

       2,498 TONS (STANDARD)

LENGTH—   233'

BEAM—   34'6"

DRAFT—   16'

AO-WOLLIN   1916

DISPLACEMENT—

       3,429 TONS (STANDARD)

LENGTH—   246'

BEAM—   36'

30–40 AO FOR HARBOR USE—NO DATA

AE-LAUTING, OTTER, RHEIN
(MINE TRANSPORTS)   1934

DISPLACEMENT—

       1,253 (STANDARD)

DESIGNED SPEED—9.5 KNOTS

4 OTHERS—NO DATA

ACL-ex-TARONGA   1934

DISPLACEMENT— 7,003 TONS (GROSS)
LENGTH—   484' OA
BEAM—   61'3"
DRAFT—   29' (FULL LOAD)
DESIGNED HP—   8,000
DESIGNED SPEED—17 KNOTS
ENDURANCE—   15,000 MILES (AT MAX. SUSTAINED SPEED)
ARMAMENT—   ?2-5"9 ?-4"1, AAMG

AP-TRANSPORTS

K—1–6—NO DATA GIVEN

ACL-TULANE   1940

DISPLACEMENT— 5,485 TONS (GROSS)
LENGTH—   432'8" OA
BEAM—   57'3"
DRAFT—   25'7" (FULL LOAD)
DESIGNED SPEED—16 KNOTS
ENDURANCE—   ?15,000 MILES (AT MAX. SUSTAINED SPEED)
ARMAMENT—   ?2-5"9 ?-4"1, +AAMG

ACL-BOCKENHEIM   1929

DISPLACEMENT—
       7,019 TONS (GROSS)
DESIGNED HP— 5,500
SPEED—   15–16 KNOTS (MEAN ON TRIAL)
ENDURANCE—   15,000 MILES (AT MAX. SUSTAINED SPEED)
ARMAMENT—   ?2-5"9 ?-4"1, AAMG

ACL-ex-TEMPLAR   1929

DISPLACEMENT— 6,728 TONS (GROSS)
LENGTH—   461'4" OA
BEAM—   60'6"
DRAFT—   29' (FULL LOAD)
DESIGNED HP—   5,400
DESIGNED SPEED—16 KNOTS
ENDURANCE—   15,000 MILES (AT MAX. SUSTAINED SPEED)
ARMAMENT—   ?2-5"9 ?-4"1, AAMG

NOTE—ALL MAY BE FITTED WITH SEARCHLIGHTS AND TORPEDO TUBES

AGS—SURVEYING VESSELS
METEOR
1924

DISPLACEMENT—	1,181 TONS (NORMAL)		
LENGTH—	220' OA	BEAM—	31'
DRAFT—	10'1" (MAXIMUM)		
DESIGNED HP—	1,650	DESIGNED SPEED—14 KNOTS	
ENDURANCE—	6,000 MILES AT 9 KNOTS		
ARMAMENT—	1-3".4 AA		

NORDEROOG, SÜDEROOG
1911-12

DISPLACEMENT—	89 TONS (NORMAL)
LENGTH—	74'10" OA
BEAM—	15'8"
DRAFT—	4'7" (MAXIMUM)
DESIGNED HP—	130
DESIGNED SPEED—8.8 KNOTS	

TRITON
1920

DISPLACEMENT—	1,005 TONS (STANDARD)
LENGTH—	217' OA
BEAM—	32'10"
DRAFT—	13'1" (MAXIMUM)

HOOGE
1940

DISPLACEMENT—	2,000 TONS (STANDARD)

AG—GUNNERY SCHOOL VESSELS
C.16—1905   C.9-10—1907   C.5—1908   C.3—1909   C.14—1913   C.1

DISPLACEMENT—	80 TONS (NORMAL)		
LENGTH—	60' OA	BEAM—	16'6"
DRAFT—	6'		
DESIGNED HP—	150	DESIGNED SPEED—9 KNOTS	
FITTED FOR ELECTRIC-MINE DETONATION			

MINING VESSELS AND BARRAGE CRAFT
M.T. 1, M.T. 2   1917

DISPLACEMENT—	550 TONS (NORMAL)		
LENGTH—	172'8" OA	BEAM—	29'6"
DRAFT—	7'		
DESIGNED HP—	370	DESIGNED SPEED—10 KNOTS	
ENDURANCE—	1,200 AT 7 KNOTS	MINES—	?30

DRACHE
1908

DISPLACEMENT—	790 TONS (NORMAL)		
LENGTH—	177'2" (PP)	BEAM—	29'6"
DRAFT—	9'10" (MAXIMUM)		
DESIGNED HP—	2,200	DESIGNED SPEED—15 KNOTS	
ARMAMENT—	4-4".1—6 SMALL GUNS		

65 BARRAGE CRAFT —NO DATA

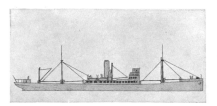

FISHERY PROTECTION VESSELS

WESER, ELBE   1931

DISPLACEMENT—   591 TONS (NORMAL)

LENGTH—   168'11" OA
                 (WESER-184'?)

BEAM—   27'3"

DRAFT—   10'7" (MAXIMUM)

DESIGNED HP—   1,600

DESIGNED SPEED—15 KNOTS

ENDURANCE—   7,000 MILES AT
                 11.5 KNOTS

ARMAMENT—   1-3".5 45 CAL

GUNNERY SCHOOL VESSELS

AMMON   1922

DISPLACEMENT—
                 7,134 TONS (GROSS)

LENGTH—   438'4" OA

BEAM—   25'8" (MAX)

DES SPEED—   12.5 KNOTS

NIXE (YACHT)   1914

DISPLACEMENT—
                 106 TONS (NORMAL)

DESIGNED HP—
                 210

SLOOP (AVISO)
HELA   1940

KREUZER, DAHME—NO DATA

TORPEDO SCHOOL TENDERS

ORKAN   1916
DISPLACEMENT—   470 TONS (NORMAL)
LENGTH—   120' OA
BEAM—   24'
DRAFT—   12'6" (MAXIMUM)
DESIGNED HP—   400
DESIGNED SPEED—10 KNOTS

JAEGER—NO DATA GIVEN

GUNNERY TRAINING VESSELS
MARS   1937
DISPLACEMENT—   2,414 TONS (GROSS)
LENGTH—   324'4" OA
BEAM—   46'11"
DRAFT—   18'2" (MAXIMUM)

CARL ZEISS   1926
DISPLACEMENT— 1,701 TONS (GROSS)
DESIGNED SPEED—10 KNOTS

JUPITER—NO DATA GIVEN

TARGET VESSELS

AHRENSBURG   1939
DISPLACEMENT—   3,200 TONS (GROSS)
LENGTH—   315' OA
BEAM—   46'5"
DRAFT—   28'1" (MAXIMUM)
DESIGNED SPEED—16 KNOTS

ANGELBURG   1938
DISPLACEMENT—   3,040 TONS (GROSS)
LENGTH—   325' OA
BEAM—   45'8"
DRAFT—   26'1" (MAXIMUM)
DESIGNED HP—   3,200
DESIGNED SPEED—15 KNOTS

HERTHA   1905
DISPLACEMENT—   1,221 TONS (GROSS)
LENGTH—   250'2" OA
BEAM—   34'
DRAFT—   13'3" (MAXIMUM)
DESIGNED HP—   2,600

TARGET SERVICE SHIPS
HESSEN (ex-OBB)   9/19/05
DISPLACEMENT—   12,988 TONS (NORMAL)
LENGTH—   419' OA PLUS NEW BOW   BEAM—72'10" DRAFT—25'3" (MAXIMUM)
DESIGNED HP—   16,000   DESIGNED SPEED—18 KNOTS
ENDURANCE—   6,340 MILES @ 10 KNOTS, 2,570 @ 15 KNOTS

ZÄHRINGEN (ex-OBB)   1901